FRIDAYS
WITH
BILL

To Rob and Nancy,

In Bill and Brady we trust

all the best

John

FRIDAYS WITH BILL

INSIDE THE FOOTBALL MIND OF BILL BELICHICK

John Powers

TRIUMPH
BOOKS

Library of Congress Cataloging-in-Publication Data

Names: Powers, John, 1948- author.
Title: Fridays with Bill : inside the football mind of Bill Belichick / John Powers.
Description: Chicago, Illinois : Triumph Books LLC, [2018]
Identifiers: LCCN 2018023881 | ISBN 9781629376295
Subjects: LCSH: Belichick, Bill—Quotations. | Football coaches—United States—Quotations. | Coaching (Athletics)—Philosophy.
Classification: LCC GV959 .P68 2018 | DDC 796.332092 [B]—dc23
    LC record available at https://lccn.loc.gov/2018023881

This book is available in quantity at special discounts for your group or organization. For further information, contact:

Triumph Books LLC
814 North Franklin Street
Chicago, Illinois 60610
(312) 337-0747
www.triumphbooks.com

Printed in U.S.A.
ISBN:978-1-62937-629-5
Design by Meghan Grammer

Bill Belichick's observations throughout the text were taken directly from his Friday press conferences. They were condensed for purposes of space and clarity. The photographs are provided courtesy of *The Boston Globe*.

*To George, who was present at the creation
of both the Patriots and my career.*

CONTENTS

INTRODUCTION

PATRIOTS COACH BILL BELICHICK IS FAMOUS FOR PRESS conferences that are circumscribed and laconic. First, there'll be a brief look back at the previous game: "We're on to Cincinnati."

This usually will be followed by a terse explanation of decisions. Question: "For those of us who weren't there last night, can you update us on why Vince Wilfork didn't play?" Answer: "We just didn't put him in. That's why." Question: "Because?" Answer: "Because there were other players who played."

Finally, a thorough scouting report on the upcoming opponent, which invariably Belichick feels will pose a stiff challenge. And, upon request, specific and detailed assessments of individual players.

But the tone and content of Friday's sessions are distinctly different. The weekly preparations for Sunday's

Belichick at the lectern for his daily briefing at Gillette Stadium during last year's training camp. (photo by John Tlumacki)

game essentially are complete: "We're winding down for the Steelers." Practices now are about fine-tuning. The midweek media crowd has dwindled to those regulars whom Belichick calls the Friday Warriors, most of whom have covered the club daily for years and whom Belichick has dubbed "the few, the proud, not the free."

"How are you guys doing?" the coach will inquire after arriving at the workroom podium in his usual cutoff hoodie. "Hay in the barn? Are those weekend stories written? All right, whatever you need here."

What ensues is the most provocative and entertaining gathering of the week, as Belichick, unusually expansive and eclectic, serves up what he apologetically acknowledges can be "long answers to short questions."

Fridays with Bill provides an intriguing glimpse into the best football mind in professional football, insights and musings from the man who has won an unprecedented five Super Bowl championships as head coach and who is destined for the Hall of Fame. This is Belichick at his most relaxed, profoundly philosophical and often puckish, holding forth on topics ranging from deferring the coin toss to his struggles with technology to his favorite

The coach pondering a question from the beat reporters during the 2006 season. (photo by Matthew Lee)

Halloween candy.

"That's a great question," is his prompt to offer a Football 101 tutorial that provides a rare glimpse into the coaching philosophy that has created the National Football League's most enduring dynasty. Belichick's topics include everything from composing rosters to developing rookies to preparing for unfamiliar rivals to challenging officials' calls on the field.

Fridays with Bill includes dozens of photographs displaying a startling variety of expressions from the league's most impassive countenance. It's a book designed both for browsing through chapters that range from assembling a roster to conducting training camp to preparing for opponents and for an intensive seminar on the art of instructing and evaluating players. For pro football fans and followers, it's a front-row seat in the Gillette Stadium media workroom—no credential required.

— ***John Powers***
April 2018

CHAPTER 1

Coaching

COACHING IS IN BILL BELICHICK'S DNA. FOR MORE than three decades, his father, Steve, was an assistant and scout at the U.S. Naval Academy and was his son's foremost mentor. "My dad…was a constant," said Belichick, whose first football job was at his father's summer camp.

While the younger Belichick was much better at lacrosse, he had an obsessive passion for the gridiron and would have worked for free if it had given him an opportunity to immerse himself in the game. The first paid position came his way in 1975, when the Baltimore Colts hired him at 23 as a special assistant for $25 a week. "I didn't know anything," he acknowledged, "but at least I was a warm body."

In his first five years, Belichick worked for four NFL clubs, usually as a special teams assistant. "I got a lot of

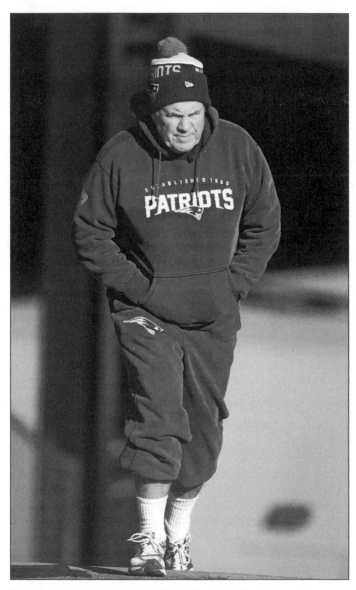

The Hoodie in winter, topped by official knit hat. (photo by Jonathan Wiggs)

exposure in a short time to a lot of football," he said. "In the end, that's not a bad thing."

Belichick collected his first two Super Bowl rings as defensive coordinator for the Giants, where he worked for a dozen years before obtaining his first head job with the Browns, who fired him after four losing seasons, just before they decamped for Baltimore. His renaissance began in 2000 in New England, where his exhaustive preparation, his absolute focus on the moment, and his unsentimental approach to his roster have produced five NFL titles and guaranteed him a place in the Hall of Fame.

"I like football. I like the game, I like the players, I like what it's all about," Belichick said. "Every part of it—whether it's assembling a team, working with new players, working with veteran players that are experienced and extremely talented at the highest level, game planning, scouting, preparation, practices, games. I enjoy all of it. It beats working."

SUMMER JOB

"I was fortunate that I was able to work at my dad's football camps, which was two to three weeks over the summer. It was a great experience for me. It was a summer job that was a week off from my other summer jobs, whether that was waiting or working for Mayflower

Moving or whatever it happened to be. It was good because I had an opportunity to work with a lot of college coaches, other guys who eventually became pro coaches. A couple coaches like Ralph Hawkins and George Boutselis, [who] I actually worked with my first year at the Colts, worked in my dad's camps, Whitey Dovell also. There were three of them on that staff.

"That was a great opportunity for me, too, to work in those camps. It was a lot of good coaches, working with kids in high school, junior high school. Not that I was like a full-fledged coach or anything, but just the experience of being around it, seeing a lot of the things, hearing coaches talk, exchanging ideas, seeing different coaches coach different techniques at the same position. It was a great experience, too. It wasn't a high-paying summer job, but it was a good job. Glad I had it."

APPRENTICESHIP

"I was playing lacrosse and that was probably my better sport. But I loved football and then when the opportunity came up to go with Coach [Lou] Holtz down to [North Carolina] State in the spring of '75, that was something I felt would marry well with my education, trying to get a master's and coach with him. When that didn't work out—Lou was the first coach that hired me and the first coach that fired me, as I like to remind him—then it fortunately worked out with Coach [Ted] Marchibroda at the Colts.

"I didn't really have anything. I didn't really have anywhere to go at that point because the N.C. State thing fell through. I was totally open and fortunately that was able to work out with Ted, and, as I said, some of the other coaches that were on that staff like George and Whitey. They were able to recommend me. [Along with] Jerry Falls, who my dad coached and who was Ted Marchibroda's son's coach in high school. So all those connections helped me get started. Plus, I think the price was right."

FIRST SEASON WITH COLTS

After sending out 250 letters seeking his first paying football job, Belichick was offered a position with the Colts, essentially viewing film and running errands. "He was willing to work 'round the clock for nothing and learn everything he could about the game," recalled head coach Ted Marchibroda. While Belichick earned a pittance, it was a priceless chance to study the NFL from the bottom up.

"We went to camp July 5. The first game was September 21, I think. So, six preseason games, three scrimmages against the Redskins. It was a whole two and a half months of training camp basically before we even played a game. It was a long, long preseason. Squads were small, so I snapped a lot to help the timing for the offense, passing, 7-on-7 and 1-on-1 drills, things like that. It was a great experience with Coach [Ted] Marchibroda and [defensive coordinator] Maxie Baughan and the rest of the defensive staff, and George Boutselis, the special teams coach.

"I learned an awful lot. I didn't know anything. I was just thrown into an environment where I think there were only seven coaches on the staff. Three on offense, three on defense, and one on special teams. I was like the eighth guy. I didn't know anything but at least I was a warm body. I got thrown a lot of responsibility and opportunity to do things that, had there been a bigger staff, I would have never gotten to do. That was a great opportunity for me. We started out 1–4, playing in front of 20,000 people there at Memorial Stadium.

"Then we started winning and Bert Jones had a tremendous year—we had a real good defense. The front four there of Fred Cook, Joe Ehrmann, Mike Barnes, and John Dutton, they had like 50-something sacks that year. We won our last nine games. We went from 1–4 to 10–4. We went from playing in front of 20,000 to whatever that holds, 60-some. So that was pretty exciting. We lost to Pittsburgh in the playoff game—they eventually won the Super Bowl.

"[We] started training camp at Goucher College and we were there until the first of September. Then we went from Goucher to McDonogh School and practiced out in the pasture there. It was crazy. We were there for a couple weeks then finally the Orioles finished up. They were in the World Series that year, I think, so we didn't even get to Memorial Stadium until around the first of October. Of course, at that point the infield was still down. They resodded that, so we only practiced on half the field and had about 40 yards to practice on. That wore out pretty quickly, so then we would go across the street to Eastern High School and practice.

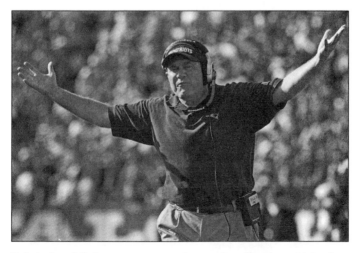

Belichick in full dyspepsia, appealing to the officials amid the first defeat of the 2011 season at Buffalo. (photo by Barry Chin)

"The whole team walks out of Memorial Stadium, hits the 'WALK' button, goes across 33rd Street, and walks over to Eastern High School, which had two blades of grass—dirt, glass, rocks. It was an inner-city practice field, about what you'd expect, filming from a stepladder. But it worked. Team started slow, gained a lot of confidence and came together. That was a really good football team. Bert Jones was a great quarterback and he continued to be until he hurt his shoulder. There's no telling how good that guy would have been. If he'd had a full career, he could have been up there with anybody I've been around, certainly. I learned a lot. I didn't put a lot of money in the bank but in terms of experience I did, not actual cash. That was a fun year."

EARLY YEARS AS PRO ASSISTANT

"I was very fortunate my first few years in the league. I worked for a lot of different coaches, worked with a lot of different assistant coaches, worked in different systems, worked in different cities, a lot of different players, different organizations. So I got a lot of exposure, a lot more than I wanted, but I got a lot of exposure in a short amount of time to a lot of football. In the end, that's not a bad thing. Wasn't great at the time, but in the end it turned out to be beneficial."

STEELERS

The Steelers of the mid-to-late '70s were a muscular and color-ful dynasty that won four Super Bowls in six seasons and sent nine players to the Hall of Fame, along with Coach Chuck Noll. The Steel Curtain, their defensive line that was anchored by "Mean" Joe Greene, set the tone for a smashmouth club that still plays old-school football.

"In '75 with the Colts, we started out 1–4 and we won the last nine games to go 10–4 and win the division. It was a tremendous turnaround. Then we went to Pittsburgh for the playoffs and they had a great team. We really had a chance in that game. It was like 17–13 in the fourth quarter. We drive down, we're on the five- or six-yard line and they intercepted, ran it back for a touchdown. So instead of going ahead now we're down by two scores and we end up getting beat.

"The point being, for my first year in the league, just seeing how good they were. I mean, they were so good on defense. Every guy was better than the next guy. From Joe Greene to Jack Lambert, that whole front four, and then the secondary. And offensively....

"When you're a young coach and you're [think-ing,] 'Okay, who does things in a way that you admire or respect or want to emulate?' Or, 'What can you take from a good program to help you as a coach?' Or, 'If you ever get a chance, what would you do that they do?' They were one of those teams. From the first year the Steelers had a very strong impact from the outside on my philosophy as a coach."

EXCHANGING IDEAS

"You talk to a lot of people. It depends on what kind of information you're looking for. If it's another team or someone that's familiar with that team or a player and they're familiar with that player, that's one thing. And if

The coach clarifying before the next play against Pittsburgh in 2013. "You want everybody to be on the same page doing the right thing." (photo by Jim Davis)

they're not or they're not as familiar with it as somebody else, it's, 'Who do you ask the questions to?' Somebody to give you the answers you're looking for. It depends on what you're after."

VISITING COLLEGE COACHES

Each year, Belichick hits the road to check in with college coaches and evaluate players that the Patriots might be interested in drafting. This year's itinerary took him to Alabama, North Carolina State, South Carolina, Georgia, and Ohio State.

"That's one of the great things about going out in spring, going to talk to Coach [Nick] Saban or Coach [Urban] Meyer, wherever the travels take you to. It's just interesting to watch somebody else run their practice, how they set up the drills, how they break it down timewise, different things like that. So, that's good.

"A lot of times you talk to people about that and say, 'Hey, how do you handle this? How do you handle that?' You're always looking for better ways to do things and how you can best teach and instruct your players and team most efficiently. We're always striving to improve that. We talk about it every year. What's our meeting time? How do we break that up? What's our practice time? How do we break that up? What's our walk-through time? When do we watch film? How do we do that? How can we do it better? Should we do it more together? Should we do it in different groups? Should we change the structure of the groups? How much should players watch by themselves? How much should they watch with the coach? How much should they... you know, all those different kinds of things. That's a continuous self-evaluation that you do as a team to try and find the best way to do things."

HEAD COACH'S OVERALL RESPONSIBILITY

"There's no set formula for me. I try to coach the entire team because that's what I'm responsible for. The assistant coaches do a great job in each of their areas, but part of my responsibility is to coordinate the whole thing—offense, defense, special teams, and any other elements of the team that come into it, the conditioning, training and preparation, and so forth. That's really what my job is.

"It varies from day to day, year to year, situation to situation, where that time is spent. But whatever I do is where I feel I can be the most efficient and help the team the most. Part of that is organizational, making sure that everybody is in a position where they can do their job and be productive in what they're being asked to do, that they have enough time to do it, that they have the resources to do it, whatever it happens to be. It's not 'do this' or 'do that,' it's ultimately 'do everything,' and let the coaches and other people on our staff do their job and handle their responsibilities and try to make sure that it all sort of fits together and we look like we halfway know what we're doing."

DECISION-MAKING

"What I try to do is make decisions that are the best for our football team. And some of them are hard, some of them are pretty obvious, but in the end I try to do what's best for the team and that excludes personal feelings and personal relationships. We're in a very competitive sport, competitive environment. We all understand that. It's based on performance and that performance is week to week and year to year."

COACHING A NEW TEAM

"Sometimes a coach comes up from within his own organization. But when you come into a new organization you try to get things in a way that either you're used to or you're comfortable with as a head coach. All the support people that are involved in that are important components, too, because they interact so closely with the coaching staff and the players and the team—trainers, doctors, video people, equipment people, grounds crews, so forth and so on. There are a lot of moving parts in and around the team.

"So trying to get all of that coordinated and done in a way that is really efficient so you don't feel like you're wasting a lot of time on things that in the past were pretty smooth for you wherever you were before. It feels like you're having time taken away from football, the team, and preparation to deal with all of these other things. So that's one thing. The other thing is just trying to institute your program, what you believe in, the way you want to play the game, your plays, your philosophy, your practice

Belichick confers with Matt Patricia, his longtime defensive coordinator and present Detroit head coach, during the 2016 AFC title victory over the Steelers. (photo by Barry Chin)

tempo. Just all the little things that in some way or another in the big picture are all connected. It might seem like it is one little isolated thing on a team, but when you tie that into a lot of other things that are going on it can be an important component of the whole team-building process. Trying to get all those things to work properly and efficiently, that's a challenge, too."

AFTER THE FIRST YEAR

Belichick was head coach in Cleveland from 1991 through 1995, and was dismissed after four losing seasons. Though he wasn't hired as Patriots head coach until after Pete Carroll was fired in 1999, he did spend a year in Foxborough as Bill Parcells' assistant in 1996.

"In some respects it's easier to coach the team after the first year. The first year, a lot of times there's an adjustment or a transition depending on what happened previously. In succeeding years at least you have the ability to build off of some kind of base. Each year brings its own challenges. I think that's the way it will always be. There are always new things. Every team changes somewhere along the line—players, coaches, situations, schedule, opponents, conditions.

"There is always change and, to a certain degree, you have to go back and rebuild that every single year. That is what training camp is for, that's what preseason games are for, that's what practice is for, is to just continue to build that up brick by brick and get your team prepared for it, to deal with it this year, not just because it happened in the past. That ensures that you'll handle it correctly or well this time or the next time it comes up."

LOYALTY

"I feel a loyalty to all the people that are in the organization. And I'm not saying I'm great or anything, that's not the point. The point is, when you're the head coach, there are a lot of people that are dependent on you. Having been an assistant coach for a long time and been the son of an assistant coach for a long time, you know that your future is, to a certain degree, tied to the head coach. It's important to me to be able to hopefully provide some stability to the other members of the coaching staff, the members of the organization that relate to the football department, the players. We all know that the first thing that changes is the coach; the next thing is most of the roster.

"I certainly like the fact that we have players that have been brought up in this system, that have tried to develop in this system and hopefully they have the confidence to know that they can come back and play in this system again with the skills and the training and the knowledge that they've learned to do it. I feel a loyalty to them and I think that they also feel a loyalty to me along those same lines. It's a two-way street. I know everybody has got to take care of themselves and their own needs and all that.

"I do have a lot of loyalty and respect for the people who work for me and I want to try to continue to provide a good working environment for them to be successful, for us to be successful, so that we can all benefit from that. So, yeah, I would say that's definitely important to me. That's the way I was brought up. I mean, when you're an assistant coach and the head coach isn't there, you're probably not going to be there, either. That's just the way it is. I learned that a long time ago."

STAFF CONTINUITY

"We're very blessed here to have the group of guys that we have on our staff. They have their position groups and their players ready to go each and every week. On a short week it's even more critical for that communication to be exactly the way that we need it to be so they can learn the game plan and adjust to the things we're asking them to do in a short period of time. They each have a lot of different responsibilities relative to presenting the scouting report, the game-plan information, the installation, the tips and pointers for each player and each position group. I've got a tremendous amount of trust and faith in those guys. They do a tremendous job with their group of guys and I think it shows on the field."

SMALLER STAFFS

"I've always thought that the smaller staff is a little bit easier for me to handle and the coaches that I've worked with, particularly Bill Parcells, certainly lived with a small staff. I know my first year with the Baltimore Colts we had only seven assistant coaches and a lot of teams in the league had double digits, 12 or 13. When you have 20-something coaches, it's hard to get all of those people on the same page, let alone to get all the players to have that kind of consistency. When you have one coach responsible for a group instead of two or three it's easier to get the kind of consistency and communication that you need within that group. So that's why I do it that way. That's how I was brought up and that's what I know, and I guess I'm comfortable with it. I'm sure other coaches have other ways of doing it and have good reasons and they're very good and they do a great job, too. I'm not saying it's the right way. It's just our way."

CHALLENGES AND
REWARDS OF COORDINATORS

"It's the performance of your unit. Certainly the performance of the team is important, but if you're an offensive coordinator you really don't have much input in the kicking game or defense.... I'd say the most rewarding thing is to see your unit improve and develop and play competitively and successfully out on the field. The most challenging aspect of it is getting them to do that."

For some die-hard fans, the devotion to the head coach literally is skin-deep. (photo by Pat Greenhouse)

ASSISTANT COACHES' DUTIES

Belichick had a lengthy and varied apprenticeship before he became a head coach, spending 16 years as an assistant with the Colts, Lions, Broncos, and Giants. While he spent almost all of that time working on defense and special teams, he was employed by Detroit for a season as receivers coach. After Belichick was cut loose by the Browns, he spent another four years as Bill Parcells' assistant head coach with the Patriots and Jets.

"It's something that definitely goes under the radar for the most part, but when you're an assistant coach you have the players that you're coaching and you have X number of plays and it's an important decision how you distribute those plays—which players get which plays, how many they get, the exact ones they do get in terms of their preparation. You can't run everything and everybody can't take all the plays.

"The [plays] that you give to the various players, there should be a reason for them and some type of rotation that gives everybody work and everybody improves. But you've got to be selective as to who does what, who's in with who and who takes which plays. And, again, that can have a lot to do with the preparation of the players and the team. When you get to the end of the week and you get into a game and you call a play and the guy hasn't run that play in practice because another guy ran it—whatever the reasons were—that can affect your timing and so forth.

"So those are really little decisions, but they're big decisions and they're critical decisions, and those are the ones that the assistant coaches [make]. You have to get everybody ready but you also have to get the guys that you think are going to be doing it sure that they can do it. And that's what a good assistant does at any position."

SHARED CHARACTERISTICS BETWEEN COACHES AND SCOUTS

"I do think that a person that is good at scouting and is good at coaching is a better coach or a better scout than somebody who is just one or the other, because it gives you better understanding. If you scout players and you understand the scheme that they're playing in it's a little bit easier to understand what the player's doing rather than just watching his physical skills.

"You can watch him play the game and say, 'Okay, you know in this situation this is really what he should be doing.' You're sure that's what he's being coached to do. Maybe you can figure out which guy is making a mistake when there is a mistake made. If you have a good under-standing of schemes and football—a coaching Xs-and-Os kind of background—and at the same time when you're

The coach signing a variety of football keepsakes during last year's training camp. (photo by John Tlumacki)

coaching and you're making out game plans and you're trying to evaluate the other team, if you're really good at evaluating players and picking out their strengths and weaknesses, then that can help you attack or defend what your opponents are doing there.

"I think that's a good combination. Sometimes coaches get into a comfort zone with players who just know what to do, who know their assignments, and there's a comfort level there because you know the guy is not going to go out there and [mess] it up…. Sometimes scouts see it the other way around. They see a guy with more talent but don't take in to account the experience or the overall instinctiveness, that a player with a little less talent could be a better football player because of his instincts and his intangibles and things like that, than a guy who can run a little faster and jump a little higher. Again, there's a balance there because both things are important."

APPROACHING A NEW SEASON

Belichick has worked as an NFL coach for 43 seasons. Not only has he never held a job outside of the league, he also never has been unemployed.

"We've always taken the approach that every year is a new season and last year is last year. The slate is wiped clean for all of us—rookies, veterans, coaches, experienced or inexperienced. We're all starting all over again and we all need to build a good base, build a good foundation, reestablish our level of performance in the next season. It's been six months since any of us have played or coached competitively and we all need to go through the same process of fine-tuning our skills and bringing the team together as one collective unit. That includes all those people—players, coaches, play callers, coordinators, trainers, all the people involved in the game-day operations.

"This year is its own entity and you start all over again from scratch. That's the way we've always approached it. We've had successful seasons and we've had other seasons that didn't end the way we wanted them to, but the following year we've tried to take that approach. Certainly you come into the season with a good level of confidence after having a successful season the year before, but I think we're all mature enough to realize that it's a new year. You can look at the standings from last year and the year before and year before that and you see teams go from the bottom to the top and you see them go from the top down the line…. One year the Dolphins were, whatever it was, 1–15, and the next year they won the division. We see that pretty regularly in the NFL now, those types of examples."

Wherever he is on the practice field, Belichick is the central figure. (photo by Jonathan Wiggs)

MARCHING ORDERS

"Let's say we start the season in April. We sit down with that player and say, 'Okay, here's what we want you to do in the off-season program—weight, conditioning, technique, position, whatever it is. Here's what we want you to concentrate on.' We get to the end of that we say, 'Okay, here was your off-season. You did this well, you need to do a better job of this.' Okay, now we're heading into training camp, 'Here's what we want you to do—this, this, this, and that.' We get to the end of training camp, 'Okay, you did a good job on this, you still need to work on that. This is better, or this still needs to be improved.' We get to somewhere in the midpoint of the season and we sit down and have the same conversation. 'Look, this is what we told you at the beginning of the year. You've done a great job with this, you still need to do better at this, this, and that—here's what you need to do.'

"Injuries may play a part in some of those discussions. We get somewhere close to the end of the year, all right, we have X number of weeks to go. 'Here's what we need from you the last three weeks, four weeks, whatever it is. Here's what you need to concentrate on. You did a great job on this, that, and the other thing. Here's what you need to do.'

"So we do it on a regular basis. We're not going to sit around here and waste a whole year and then say, 'Okay, let's have a meeting.' We're not going to have a meeting every day, but there are certainly different parts of the year where you can. We do it for the entire team. It's each individual player, it's each coach, each position, each unit. Offense, defense, special teams, running game, passing game, kickoff return, punt coverage, whatever it is. We evaluate those at various points and say, 'Okay, how are we doing? We're all right on this, we're not so good on this, we need to make this change, whatever.' We're our own R&D team. We can't hire some consultant to come in here like a company can do and, 'All right, let's take a look at this and you guys do a study on that and tell us this, tell us that.' Who's going to do that?"

PLANNING PRACTICES

"We talk each day about what the team needs. We have a basic structure of, this is what we do, but we change that depending on what we feel our needs are. Definitely a big part of it is health and the overall readiness of the team. That's very subjective, obviously, but we do the best we can in consultation with the training staff, the strength and conditioning staff, position coaches. A lot of times they have a good tempo of where their individual group or particular players are and sometimes that affects the rest of the preparation."

EVALUATING INDIVIDUAL PERFORMANCE

"In the end the bottom line is, how do you feel the player's production on any given play is rated towards the potential? Or what he could have done or he should have been able to do in that particular situation? That doesn't mean every play has to be an 80-yard touchdown. It just means, given what happened on the play, what is the most you could have expected from him and did you get that? Did you get less or was there a critical mistake that really put the team in a tough situation or put another player in a tough situation?… Sometimes [you have to say about] certain players in certain games, 'Well, they didn't really have many chances in that game,' or 'It's really hard to evaluate them in that particular game because there just weren't a lot of opportunities.'"

EVALUATING LINEMEN

"You can evaluate what you're teaching them to do. Do they understand the plays? Do they understand their assignments? Are they using the proper technique in their assignment? Can you evaluate whether a guy can power rush or whether you can stop a power rush or whether you can stop the physical play or block physical players in there? No, and we don't want to evaluate that. That's not what this is for. In terms of evaluation, it's definitely limited. What we do want is that players understand their assignments, their techniques, adjustments that they're going to have to make so that when we can evaluate it they already know what to do and there's not a lot of 'Do I do this? Do I do that?' hesitation, which nobody looks good doing.

"It's hard to evaluate a player when he's not confident or sure of what he's doing. If he knows what to do and he's sure how to do it and he goes out there and does it the best that he can and the guy on the other side of the ball does the same thing, then you can see what you have."

PRIORITIZING INSTRUCTIONS

"You always want to prioritize what's important because by the end of the week we're sitting here on Friday or Saturday and every player has been told 1,000 times: 'Do this, do that.' 'When this happens, do this, when that happens, do that.' 'If they do this, you're going to check to that.' 'Read this guy, read that guy.'

"There's got to be some kind of priority…. You want to bring it back to what are the most important things to do as a team and at each position…. You remind them that this is how the game is played. This is what your role is. This is what your job is. First things first."

MISTAKES

"We're all going to make mistakes and nobody makes more of them than I do. I understand that mistakes are part of the game. I've been in it long enough to know there's no perfect player, no perfect game or practice. If you go out there and compete against high-level competition they're going to make some plays, too. But there's below the line and we just can't live with that and expect to win. That's the bottom line… if you're playing defensive back you can't have a ball thrown over your head for an 80-yard touchdown. It's not acceptable.

"I don't care if the guy is a Hall of Fame player or if he's a rookie free agent in his first practice. We can't play like that. We can't throw a pass into a team meeting where there's four defenders there and try to jam the ball in there and get it picked off when they have four guys standing there. It's unacceptable. We can't win doing that. I don't care who the quarterback is, it doesn't make any difference. We can't jump offside and false start and be in first-and-15 and first-and-5 and let them convert third downs and third-and-4 because we jump offside. You can't play like that. It doesn't matter who the player is, it's still below the line. We just can't play like that and expect to win with those kinds of mistakes.

"Now, is that going to happen? Yeah, it's going to happen, sure. I understand that. But if it happens too often, we can't play like that. And there's a new coach up here, too, if it happens too often. I know that, too. The things that cause you to lose, you have to eliminate. Before you can win, you can't lose. When you do things as a coach or as a player that cause you to lose then you won't be in this job long."

IDENTIFYING BREAKDOWNS

"My advice to you and to the fans and to everybody else would be: [don't] be too quick to decide who's right and who's wrong when you don't really know what's going on. And that's hard for me, too. If I watch something on another team, I can see there's a mistake. I'm not necessarily sure who made it. Obviously, something wasn't done properly; that's evident. But what went wrong and why it went wrong, what's the background of what happened, if you're not part of the team, that's a very hard thing to evaluate. I know it's very hard for me when I see a mistake on film that another team makes to identify exactly what the problem was because it could probably be one of two or three things. Unless you actually know what the call was, what they were taught to do, I don't know if you really know who actually made the mistake."

GAME-DAY COACHING

"Number one, getting the most important things handled, whatever they are. It could be what you're doing, it could be what they're doing, it could be the weather conditions. Whatever the most important things are, making sure that you start at the top. And, also, you don't have all day. You don't even know how long you have. If you're on defense, the offense could be out there for a seven-minute drive. They could be out there for a 30-second drive. So you've got to prioritize what you're doing so that you get

Belichick with former head coach Bill Parcells before the Super Bowl showdown with the Packers. Belichick won his first two Super Bowl rings with the Giants as Parcells' defensive coordinator before rejoining him in New England as assistant head coach. (photo by Jim Davis)

to the most important things first so if you're running out of time you haven't used your time inefficiently.

"Number two, there's what we're doing versus what they're doing. A lot of times, making sure that you're right is more important than identifying what they're doing. Until you got that cleared up then you're kind of spinning your wheels in the sand, and you're not making any progress because you don't really understand exactly what the issues are. In the game situation, that [all] changes.

"You have the information from players which is, they're in the heat of battle. You have information from the press box, as much of an overview as you can get. You have sideline information. Sometimes information, you don't see it quite the same way so you've got to sort all that out. Then there is the balance of fixing what it is in the rearview mirror and looking ahead. 'Okay, we've got to take care of these problems; here's what happened.'

"But at the same time you're spending all your time on that, some of that is not even relevant, because the next time you go out there, 'Okay, what are we going to do? We've corrected those problems. Maybe we're going to make a different call or maybe we're going to be in a different situation. How do we handle that?' So there is the balance of new information versus analysis of previous information…. What information is important, where do we start, how do we get the most information across in the least amount of time and making sure that we get the information to the right people?"

GAME-DAY BUTTERFLIES

"Every year I walk out on the field before the game and I think, 'This will be a little better this year,' and it never is. I think everybody has them [butterflies] and then the ball is kicked off, you start playing, and you kind of settle into it. It's good to get that first play over with and just get into the game. But the buildup, the anxiety, and the butterflies—that's the perfect word for it because that's what they are."

PSYCHING UP

"I think in the end the games are won and lost out on the field by the players. You can go in there and beat your helmet against your locker before you go out on the field, hold hands, chant, kick chairs, and break blackboards, but as soon as the ball is snapped you do your job better than they do theirs or vice versa…. I think you can go in there, take a sledgehammer and break up the cinder blocks, but I don't think that helps you block them. I don't think it helps you tackle them. I don't think it helps you do what you need to do from a football standpoint. If you can't do that then I think the rest of that is minimal."

MANAGING EMOTIONS DURING GAMES

"Playing emotionless is not good. When you're emotional, when you have a lot of energy, you're on a higher alert, but there's a point where that can go over the edge and be detrimental to where it's more about that than it is about the execution of your job. So there is a fine line there between poise, composure, decision-making, and energy and emotion and enthusiasm. They're all good and they're all important but there is a balance there. In terms of decision-making, I think you've got to make decisions based on what's right. Not where your heart is, but what's best for the football team."

FOOTBALL VS. BASEBALL

"The difference [is] you can't run out the clock. You have to get them out. It's a tough nine outs. Joe Torre told me that and Tony La Russa verified it. You have to get them out."

NEW BEGINNINGS

"Every year is different. Every year is a great challenge, great opportunity. Every time it comes around it's nice to be able to go up to the plate, get a turn at bat."

CHAPTER 2

Players

WHAT EVERY PATRIOT LEARNS AS SOON AS HE ARRIVES in Foxborough is that there is one immutable rule: "You put the team first," said Bill Belichick. "You do your job. You do what the team needs you to do to win and that's what our team does."

Belichick wants smart and versatile players who are willing to embrace changing roles. "He's a football player," is one of the coach's highest compliments. Receivers may be transformed into defensive backs, quarterbacks into receivers. Starters may be put on special teams.

"All of us end up doing things at some point that maybe you'd rather not do, you'd rather have somebody else do," Belichick said. "You'd rather do something that you're good at but you have to do something that the team requires you to do. That's what team sport is, that's what football is."

The team's Next Man Up philosophy assumes that every player is ready to step in at any moment, just like Malcolm Butler, the obscure, undrafted cornerback whose goal-line interception in the final moments against the Seahawks saved Super Bowl XLIX.

"Everybody's got a job to do and when you're called upon to do that job, everybody's expecting you and counting on you to be ready to do it, whatever that happens to be," said Belichick. "Everybody needs to be ready to go."

The coach expressing annoyance on the sidelines during a tight home game with Buffalo in 2012. "The things that cause you to lose, you have to eliminate." (photo by Jim Davis)

DIFFERENT PERSONALITIES

"We have 53 different personalities on the team. That's probably a good thing. You don't want them all to be the same. They just have to blend in and respect each other. We all have our own personalities and I think that's great for the team as long as there's mutual respect and it's done in a respectful way within the team context. I don't try to shape or judge anybody else's personality. They are who they are.

"Different people have different styles, playing styles and emotional levels and all that kind of thing. Somehow [you create] a blend of those personalities into your team. That's what creates that team. Each team is different, unique. It's made up of different people every year and sometimes personalities are added, some aren't there and they mesh slightly or maybe not so slightly and that creates the personality of your entire team.

"I don't think there's any science to it. That's not anything I've ever tried to create—'Oh, we need this kind of personality on this team,' or 'Oh, we don't want that kind of personality on the team.' If they can blend together and be part of the team and do their job and be productive then that affects the personality of that group of players. I don't think that's a bad thing."

SCOUTING OTHER LEAGUES

"We scout every league to some degree. We scout all the players. We know where most of the players are but occasionally you find them somewhere else and we at least scout them. Not as heavily as college, where the majority of players come up from, but there are other places to look for them, whether it's the Arena League, Europe in the spring, that kind of thing."

UNKNOWN PLAYERS

"I think every team has a guy [where everyone thinks,] 'Where was he? What happened to him? How did he end up?' How does Steve Neal end up starting in this league? He never played high school or college football. I bet you just about every team we have played this year has a guy like that. It is interesting. It's a very inexact science. You have some guys come out, they are three-time All-Americans, they are All-This, they are All-That, and they never played a down in the NFL. Then you get other guys that don't play in high school, that don't play in college, they can barely play in Division Whatever, and here they are playing in the National Football League. So, it's inexact."

BASKETBALL PLAYERS

"I had many conversations with Bob Knight about that when he was at Indiana. I would say that the big thing for most basketball players is, in general, they're quicker than they are fast. When you get out there and time a lot of those guys in the 40-yard dash they're slow. They might look fast on a basketball court, but we have such a much bigger field that most of them don't have the speed to play at our level.

"They have quickness and a lot of times they have exceptional quickness. But when it just comes to straight flat-out speed that's where a lot of times in the scouting part of it the deficiencies come up. You go see a basketball player and say, 'This guy has great hands. This guy has great quickness. This guy is strong. He's competitive.' Then you time him and he runs 4.75–4.8 and you're like, 'What are you going to do with him?'"

BRINGING IN PLAYERS

Player acquisition in the NFL begins on the first day of the year and never ends. Free agents can be signed on January 1, the trading period begins in mid-March, and rookies are drafted at the end of April. Like the rest of the league's coaches, Belichick is constantly looking for players who can improve his roster and makes a point of knowing who's available.

"When you bring the player onto your team you want the player on your team. So whether it's an injury or a position change or a lack of experience, whatever it is, you feel like you can make that player work in your team or in your system. If you don't feel that way, then you shouldn't bring him on your team. That's not saying we're right on every player. We've made plenty of mistakes with players, bringing them onto the team and so forth. Every team in the league does that. That's part of the process. You try to make as few of those as possible, but it's an inexact science."

ESTABLISHING VALUE

"Each player has to establish his own value to the team in whatever form that is. Ultimately, when you put together the team, all the jobs have to be accounted for somehow. It doesn't have to be by this person or that person but somebody has to do it. Somebody has to cover kickoffs. You have to put a kickoff team out there, so who is that going to be? What group of people, what combination of people is that going to be? You figure that out and maybe that plays into the final decision. Or maybe you have that pretty well covered and it's the kickoff return team or it's short yardage and goal-line or whatever it is. In the end you have to take a look at all those things.

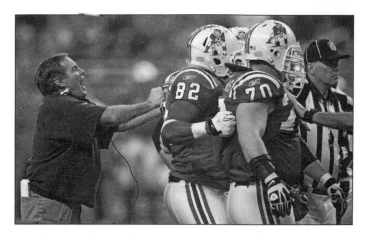

Belichick gobble-gobbling during the 2010 Thanksgiving game at Detroit while officials sort things out on the field. (photo by Matthew Lee)

"They're all factors. That's how we try to put together the team. Look at all the jobs that have to be done, try to figure out where our depth is and if there's one void there then you have to figure out how you're going to fill that. Is it change your scheme or find somebody to do it on your roster or find somebody that isn't on your roster to try to do it? Those are the issues."

TEAM FIRST

"When you sign up to play football, it's a team sport and all of us have to give up a little of our individuality or give up a little bit of what we personally like for the good of the team. And that goes for every player and every coach that's a part of this. If an athlete wants to do his individual thing then play an individual sport. Be a swimmer or play tennis or go do whatever you want as an individual sport. It's no problem. Team sports are team sports. All of us end up doing things at some point that maybe you'd rather not do, you'd rather have somebody else do.

"You'd rather do something that you're good at but you have to do something that the team requires you to do. That's what team sport is, that's what football is. You put the team first. You do your job. You do what the team needs you to do to win and that's what our team does. That's what our players do and I have a lot of respect for them. That's why they're on the team, because they have that attitude. I don't think there's anybody in this organization, player or coach, that everything's exactly the way they want it to be.

"Some things are and some things maybe you don't want to do but you have to do them because they need to be done and it's your job. You want to be part of a team, then that's part of the responsibility you accept—not only accept but embrace and understand that's what it is and you do it. A lot of people who don't understand team sports maybe can't relate to that. I don't know. When you sign up for football that's what you sign up for."

ACCEPTING ROLES

"You give up some of your individual preferences or individual control you have to play the great team game of football. If you want to go out there and run track or swim or throw the shot put or play tennis or whatever it is, great. There's nothing wrong with that and you control everything. You control how you practice. You control when you practice. You control how hard you hit the ball and how soft you hit it or whatever. Play golf. Then you're your own team, but when you buy into a team sport, not just defensively but offensively and in the kicking game, practice for the show team, practice for the other side of the ball, so forth and so on, then you make a commitment to the team."

DOING YOUR JOB

"Everybody's got a job to do and when you're called upon to do that job everybody's expecting you and counting on you to be ready to do it, whatever that happpens to be. So whether that's a player, a coach, whoever it is, things change from game to game, from year to year, and sometimes those roles change based on game plan or other situations and everybody really just needs to be ready to go. If you're a player that prepares well and your teammates count on you and you're there to deliver, whether that's one play or 60 plays or third-down plays or fourth-down plays or first-down plays, whatever they are, you just prepare. And when you get the opportunity you go in there and perform to your best level. Hopefully that's good enough.

"I think the players do a good job of that. They do a good job of preparing. They do a good job of understanding that their role might change from week to week and whatever they're asked to do, they try to do for the benefit of the team. To have a good team that's what you need. You need everybody to sacrifice some personal preferences or individual goals or however you want to look at it in order for the team to have success."

PLAYING TIME

"What players need to understand is there's only so much that they can control. There are some decisions that are coaches' decisions and playing time is one of them. All a player can do is go out there and prepare and do his best and then the coaches make the substitutions and that's their job. It's not a player's job to do that. I think the things that are in a player's control they should work hard to control them. Things that are out of their control, for the most part it's a lot of time and energy worrying about something that you don't have any control over and it's probably better that they don't get too wrapped up in that."

LEARNING STYLES

"We all learn differently, we learn at different rates. We do everything. We teach it verbally, we teach it on paper, on the blackboard—not that there's blackboards any more, but as a figure of speech. We show it on film, we walk through it and we obviously run it in practice. Some players need to see it—see it on film, see it the way it's going to look. Some players can verbally process the information and the

Tom Brady and Belichick, both bound for the Hall of Fame, savoring the proceedings in the 2014 home blowout of the Bears. (photo by Matthew Lee)

assignments. Some players need to spatially see it—'Okay, I'm here, you're there, he's there.' They actually physically need to see the relationships, the space. Sometimes it's the quarterback saying, 'Look, here's what I see, here's what you have to do.' 'Oh, okay, now that makes sense.' Sometimes you have to see it from the quarterback's vision or the quarterback has to see it from the receiver's vision.

"We use all the teaching techniques and certainly as an individual coach if you find that one technique works better with one player and another technique works better with another player, then you somehow divide your time separately or make sure you do it both ways in your presentation. I'd say that's what good coaches, good teachers do—they find ways to make sure that the students, the players in this case, are able to get and process the information. But we all have different ways and styles and rates of learning. Not everybody is the same. That's not a criticism of one way or the others. It's just the reality of it as a teacher. You have to be able to do it differently."

INDIVIDUAL MECHANICS

"Any time you look at an individual skill such as passing, kicking, punting, a golf swing, something like that, each person's physicality is a little bit different. Their mechanics may have some variation and so there are a lot of different styles. You look at the golf tour. Not every swing is exactly the same but all of those guys are pretty good.... There are certain fundamentals that are inherent in good passes, good kicks, good punts. The way that the ball is released and the angle and the spin on the ball and the delivery and so forth.... You try to teach the players the basic fundamentals and if they can adjust their mechanics in a way to improve and still feel comfortable with it then we try to do that. And if it's an adjustment that they're really not comfortable making for whatever the reasons then I think you just have to decide if you can live with what the deficiencies are in the mechanics.

"If the punts are good but they're done in a little bit of an unorthodox way and they've satisfied what you want the punter to do then you're probably going to be happy with it. If they don't and you can't change it because that's just not the makeup of the player then you're probably not going to be happy with it.... There are players that use techniques and do certain things that you wouldn't coach a player to do if you were starting him off or if you were talking to a group of players and you'd say, 'Okay, this is fundamentally the way we want to do something.' It's the exact opposite of the way that another player is doing it but the player is very successful doing it that way and so you don't change the guy who has his own way of doing it if he is successful and he's productive.

"But at the same time you wouldn't necessarily start from scratch and teach a player who has a blank slate to do it that way because fundamentally you see some flaws in it. The biggest lesson I learned was with Everson Walls when I had him with the Giants. He came from Dallas and he had a very unorthodox way of covering man-to-man. His footwork was unorthodox and his eye control was not something that you would teach. That's probably because not a lot of guys could do it. But he had his way of doing it and he could do it pretty well.

Julian Edelman, ball in hand, trots to the sideline for a bit of consultation during a 2014 victory over Miami. (photo by Jim Davis)

"One of the first things I told Everson was, 'I'm not going to try to change your style but you have to understand what your responsibilities are on the defense and you have to perform those responsibilities. But I'll give you some latitude in the technique and the style as long as you can get the job done.' He said, Okay, I fully understand that. I want to meet the responsibilities of the position on the defense on a particular call but let me do it my way and I'll get it done. I don't know if I can do it your way because I've been doing it the other way for so long. I said, that's fine, and the guy had 60 interceptions or however many it was. He did things differently than any other defensive back I coached. But he knew what he was doing. He knew where he had to compensate and generally speaking he got the job done on a very high-percentage basis."

SEEING THINGS

"There are guys that when you watch film can look at it in the classroom and look at it in a book, they'll give it to you chapter and verse, forwards and backwards. And then you get out there on the field and spatially here's the same stuff we went over in the meeting, here's the same thing we watched on film and it happens on the field and they don't recognize it or they're late to recognize it. And then there are other guys that don't understand it in the diagram. They really don't understand it. But when you get out there spatially and say, 'Okay, this guy is here,' they say 'Oh, okay.'

"We all have different ways of learning. But you get guys like [Tom] Brady and [Randy] Moss and guys like that, they get it at every level. You diagram something and they say, 'Oh, yeah, I can picture that.' You say, 'You see this play and when this guy is here, you go there.' And they say, 'Of course I would go there. What else would I do?' It just comes easy to them. They get out there on the field and they make adjustments during the game. They just instinctively know what to do. Sometimes they see it a lot quicker than the coaches do and that's good for us."

INSTINCTIVE PLAYERS

"Some guys just have a way of finding the ball. Tedy Bruschi, Mike Vrabel, Rob Ninkovich—those guys have a lot of production on the ball and it's all different—it's strip sacks, it's fumbles, it's fumble recoveries, it's interceptions, it's tipped balls. It's a whole random variety of things but somehow they just seem to find their way. You could say that the ball finds them or they find the ball."

SITUATIONAL AWARENESS

"It's being instinctive. Like a basketball player knowing when to pull up, when to drive to the hoop, when to pull up for the jump shot, when he can make it to the basket and when he can't and when to pull out. It's all that stuff. Some guys have an instinctiveness and a capacity to do that without even being coached. You run a play and say, this is what we're going to do on this play—boom, boom. Then you go out there and run a play and something happens that you didn't even talk about. Some guys will do what they're supposed to do and other guys will say, 'Well, I should do this but here's what they did so obviously I can't do that, so I adjusted into something else.' And it's the right thing to do.

"Lawrence Taylor was like that. Lawrence Taylor knew what every player on the field was doing. I'm not saying he was a coach but, 'Okay, well, I'm here, this guy's here, that guy's there, so obviously that guy's got to be over there, that guy's got to do this.' I think guys that try to memorize plays—'Okay, I run this on that play, I run that on this play, I do this on some other play.' And then it runs together and they make mistakes. Whereas, 'Okay, I run this, well of course I've got to run this because that guy's here, that guy's there and that guy's somewhere else. So where else would I be?'

The coach watching his defense protect the red zone against the Falcons in 2017. (photo by Jim Davis)

"It's just easy for them. It's just natural. Some players have a great capacity for it and other guys, you tell them to key one guy and they come off after the play and you say, 'What did that guy do?' 'Oh, I didn't see him.' 'Well, that's the guy you're keying.'

"From Day One, you ask Tom Brady what happened after a play and he'd tell you eight things that happened. 'I dropped back, the lineman flashed in front of me, the linebacker dropped wide, this guy slipped, he was over here, the other guy flashed on his side, I stepped up, this happened, that happened.' You go back and watch the film and there are eight things that he said happened and that's what happened on the play. You can see every one of them. This guy was pressed and then he backed off late, this guy rolled down.

"Like I said, Lawrence was like that, too. Lawrence would go out there, come in after the series and say, 'Coach, they're not blocking it the way you said they were going to block it. Here's what they are doing. Instead of him taking me, he's helping. I can see that guy looking for me so if I come inside the center's going to come off and he's going to pick me up.' You can look at the film and say he's right. You could never get that from the sideline."

PLAYERS IMPROVISING

"There are rules and there are things we all do but then there are things that happen on any given play or in games and situations that aren't quite the way that they are drawn up and football players have to be football players and they have to react and make decisions and improvise and do the right thing within the context of their responsibility. Every player has to do that. Things happen not quite the way they were supposed to happen or your teammate doesn't do it quite the way he was supposed to so you have to make an adjustment or he has to make an adjustment because of you.

"Within that, you try to develop consistency within the overall team, the way it's done. So there's a certain degree of that that's inherent in every player at every position. And then there's also a certain part of it that when it takes away from your responsibility, trying to anticipate or react to something a little quickly, then it can cause you a problem. So you have to find that fine line. Every player has to do that. I'm sure each player can look back and find times where, 'I was a little too aggressive on that' and other plays where, 'I knew it. I should have just hit it a little quicker.' So it's trying to find that right balance."

ADDING RESPONSIBILITIES

"Normally when we talk to a player about taking on more responsibilities, whether it's on the same side of the ball or a different side of the ball or in the kicking game, it's with the idea that those responsibilities will give him an opportunity to get on the field more and/or increase his value to the team in terms of making the roster or, again, being on the field and having a bigger role on the team. I don't think there are too many players that don't want to play, that don't want a bigger role.

"Now when you make those moves, sometimes after the player does it they don't feel comfortable or confident in taking on those responsibilities and it doesn't work out. But you usually don't know that until you've given it a try. The player and the coaches don't know that, but you go into it feeling like, 'We'll give it a shot and see how it goes,' then you evaluate it as you start to gain more information about the change. I can't say that I've ever had too much resistance on that over my career. The intent is to not only make it better for the team but to make it better for that individual player. We can all remember plenty of examples where that versatility has paid dividends for the players involved and the team. So that's the intent. Sometimes it works out, sometimes it doesn't and you go back to where you were."

REQUESTING MATCHUPS

"You definitely have the guy who comes in here and says, 'Can I get on No. 68 this week? I mean, I could kill him. Let me get over there on him.' Or, 'Let me cover so-and-so. I can really get all over this guy.' Yeah, all right. How about taking the best guy? What about that?... I would think our guys like to go up against the other team's best player. Sometimes that's part of the game plan, sometimes it isn't and that's just something we have to sort out. I don't think it's a bad thing to want to take on their best guy, but I would say we've got a lot of guys like that.... But I've definitely seen the other side of that, too. 'Even though I play over here at this position, if you put me over there against the guy on the other side of the line I think

I can have a big day against him.' Or, 'Normally I would be covering this guy but if you put me over here on this other guy who's not very good I think I can cover him.' I've seen that, too."

POOR PERFORMANCES

"Everybody that's in the National Football League has had a bad day, every coach, every player. I couldn't list anybody that hasn't. We've all been through that. We've all had days where we haven't performed well. There have been plenty of days in practice where we haven't performed well, too. It's not just unique to the game. You can go out there and not have a good practice or not have good plays in practice and that's a part of football. It's part of being a competitor, finding a way to correct the mistakes and move on and perform better in the next opportunity you get. We all face that. That happens to everybody that's involved in this game. If you play at this level of competition, there are times you're going to come up short. We're playing against other good players, good teams, good coaches every week, too. They're working just as hard as we are. They're just as talented as we are. They're going to make some plays. We're going to make some. I think that's part of it. You learn to correct your mistakes and move on."

NEGATIVE PLAYS

"Of course you don't want to see negative plays happen, but eventually they're going to happen. You do want to see how players respond to those plays—a defensive player missing a tackle or giving up a completion or a receiver dropping a ball and things like that. Look, that's unfortunately part of the game and seeing how people respond to that type of adversity or negative play [is important]. Do they go in the tank? Does one bad play become two? Does one missed block become three? Or do they bounce back and right the ship and then settle down and do a better job? That's part of the evaluation with all our players and if they play enough they all have those plays. But it is interesting. We do talk about that, about how players respond when they have a bad play. How does that affect them on the coming plays?"

GETTING PAST MISTAKES

"We go out there, we all make mistakes, we all have plays that we wish we could have over again or do better on. You regain your balance after those and do it again and try to do it a little better the next time. You don't lose your confidence, but the next time you go out there and have a high expectation, a high level of commitment to perform to the best of your ability. Inevitably you always come up a little bit short. Nobody plays a perfect game. Then you live with those, whatever the level of disappointment is, whether it's 1 percent or 50 percent, whatever it is, and then you don't lose your confidence. You go back, correct the mistakes and turn the page and move forward.

"That's where you want to be, but sometimes it's hard. When you're disappointed and you put a lot into it, those games that you lose, if you put a lot into a particular situation and it doesn't work out, well there's obviously a high level of disappointment, which there should be if you put a lot into something and it doesn't work out well. You're not just going to walk away and say, I don't care. When you say you don't care, it's when you didn't put anything into it because you really don't care. So whatever happens, you just live with it. The ones you put a lot into and they don't work out, it's harder to get over those. But that's what we all have to do."

CELEBRATING PLAYS

"These guys work hard. They work hard every day, they work hard all week, they prepare for the game. If you go out and make a good play you should be excited about it…. When you do it together as a group, you feel good with your group. The guy who scored feels good for the

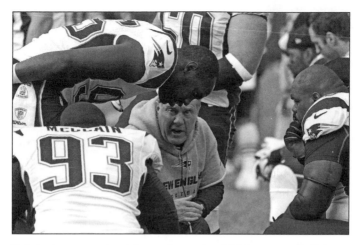

Belichick instructs the defense during the 2012 romp at Buffalo. (photo by Barry Chin)

guys who blocked for him. The guys who blocked for him feel good for the guy who scored and vice versa. You throw a pass, you catch it, somebody had to block, somebody had to run the route, somebody had to throw it, somebody else took the coverage to help somebody else get open. You intercept a pass, you had a good pass rush, other guys were covered. So there is a lot of team excitement on those plays. You see it on the sidelines. A guy on the field makes a play, you see the bench explode. That emotion naturally comes out with hard work and success. I don't think it's something you want to restrain. At the same time, there is another play. If the next play is a bad play, then that offsets it. There is a balance there in all that."

ROOKIE BONDING

"Each rookie class has a little bit of its own camaraderie and attachment to each other because they go through the whole process, the whole indoctrination, learning process and everything together. A lot of things we do, we do as an entire rookie class. All the extra meetings, whether it be football, off-field things, or personal things, they all do those together. There's a natural kind of support for each other and there's a learning thing, too, where they're sometimes more comfortable talking to each other than they are talking to a veteran and asking them a question that might be looked at as a dumb question. Whereas if you ask another rookie, he's probably in the same boat you are on something like that. It is interesting how that works."

ROOKIE EXPECTATIONS

During the Belichick era, the Patriots have had an average of eight rookies make their roster each season, the number ranging from as few as four to as many as 20. From May until training camp opens in mid-July, the first-year players attend mini-camps, development programs, a league premiere, and mandatory transition sessions to help them adjust to professional football before they start playing in earnest.

"I don't really have any expectations for any rookie players. We just coach them from the day they get here. We try to get every player to improve and learn our system and become a better football player in the NFL. That's a process. Some guys [learn] at different rates. I've learned that through a lot of experience. Some players start quickly and fizzle out. Some players start slowly and come on strong. Some players are more steady than others. You really don't know that until their rookie season is over, what the rate is or how it's all going to turn out.

"You just take it day to day, get better on a daily basis, and teach them all the things that you can teach them, get them the practice time you can practice them with, correct all the mistakes, and keep moving forward. That's what being a rookie is in the National Football League. It's a great learning experience every day, every week, and hopefully at the end of that rookie season the player has accumulated a lot of knowledge and experience and is able to use that as a good springboard for the rest of his career."

ROOKIE READINESS

"Playing a young player regardless of what position it is, there are some considerations that you have to think about. If you put a guy in too early in a situation he's not ready for, that he has almost no chance to succeed in, that's not going to do a lot for his confidence or for anybody else's confidence. That's more of a coaching error than it is a player error. He's just not ready. To put somebody in that you know is not ready to play, I think we all know what is going to happen in that situation. That really isn't fair to the player.

"Sometimes you have to do it out of necessity. Usually that's not the case. Usually you find some other alternative.... I think confidence has a lot to do with it. Some players have confidence. They could strike out every time at the plate and that wouldn't bother them. There are other guys whose confidence is a lot more fragile for whatever reason. It's hard for an athlete to achieve at a top level without a good degree of confidence... confidence to the point where he can perform to his maximum ability and that's a fine line.

"Having no confidence, we've all seen those situations where a professional golfer can barely make a three-foot putt. It's not ability. At some point it's confidence or nerves or whatever you want to call it. I think there's definitely something to that. It's hard for the coach to control the player's confidence. There's a little bit of play in there but in the end the player has to control that himself. The best way for a coach to be confident in a player is for a player to go out there and play well."

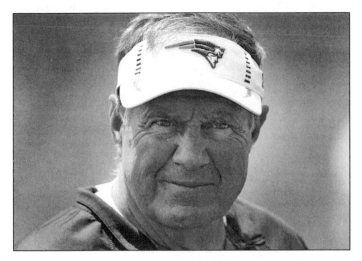

The coach, as close to ebullience as he will permit himself to come, during practice. (photo by John Tlumacki)

ROOKIE CONVERSATIONS

"We talk to them on a regular basis, I'd say at least weekly if not more. In a lot of cases it's a daily conversation with either all of them or groups of them. It's because they haven't gone through it. Everybody looking back, which I've heard many times as a coach, 'Well, I wish I had known this,' or 'I wish I had realized that,' or 'I didn't really know that.' They still don't know but at least we try to do a better job than I did back when I was with the Giants.

"You've heard that so many times from those young guys that you tell them, 'Look, this is the way it's going to be. This is what you need to be ready for. This is what's going to happen. This is how this is going to work. This is how you need to do this. This is how you need to do that.' It doesn't mean it's going to be perfect but at least they've been warned ahead of time, they have an idea of what to expect.

"A lot of times you come back and say, 'Okay, this is what we talked about. Did it happen about the way you thought it would? The way we talked about it?' 'Yeah.' 'Well, what was different?' 'I didn't expect this or I didn't expect that.' Then we talk about that and move on to the next thing. It's a long season for these guys. There are a lot of hills to climb, not just one. So it's a roller coaster. Each week is a new challenge and each day is a new challenge. I think the better you can prepare them for it, the better chance they have to meet it. But there's still no substitute for experience. Coaches, players, we try to provide that and we do that. That's every year, every group, on and off the field.

"There are a lot of things in pro football that are a lot different than college. Not just the game, not just the preparation, but once they walk out of the building there's no dormitories, no classes, not a lot of other stuff. There are a lot of other things. There's regular life to deal with, paying bills and being accountable in other areas of your life that are much less so in college. A lot of stuff that is taken care of for you or you don't have to deal with at all.

"It's the same whether you're talking to five guys, 10 guys, or 15 guys. It's the same conversation. Maybe there are more or less of them but it's the same. The five guys haven't been through it any more than the 15 guys have been through it. A lot of little things. Most of our guys aren't from this area of the country. A lot of them come from the South, some from the Midwest, some from the West. It's a different lifestyle, it's a different climate. There are a lot of things that are different up here. Just generally getting around, just doing normal things, particularly as we go deeper into the season. It's all part of the transition."

ROOKIE ROLES

"If you throw it all in there at once, sometimes that can be overwhelming and then you don't get one thing right. You try to find that balance. You take it at a pace that you think the player can handle and sometimes you're right, sometimes you're wrong and you have to adjust it one way or the other. Until you work with a guy and you're trying to do something like that with him, you have to try to figure it out on the run sometimes and that can be challenging."

ROOKIE WALL

"I don't think it affects everyone the same. The season grinds everyone down—players, coaches, experienced guys, inexperienced guys. It is a long season, it is a lot of work and you have to keep up the pace and that is challenging. For somebody who hasn't been through it before, I think it is always a little bit tougher the first year, whether it's a first-year NFL coach or a first-year NFL player. You don't really appreciate it until you actually go through it and you don't really know what you are going to go through until you are there doing it. No matter how much everyone tells you it is going to be like this or that, until you actually experience it and learn to deal with it yourself internally from a stamina and concentration standpoint I don't think you actually know exactly how to do it."

PLAYING FOOTBALL

"You just can't play football unless you play football. You can run around the track and do 500 sit-ups and jumping jacks but it's not playing football. No matter what kind of condition any athlete is in, no matter how many balls somebody throws to him or he catches, it is different when the other 21 guys are on the field and you are running a specific system against another opponent. That is all reactionary quickness, anticipation, and communication with your teammates. That's what makes football football, and there is no other way to simulate that other than to actually do it.... Conditioning is important. I am not trying to minimize that. But at the same time, you could be the greatest decathlete of all time but that doesn't mean that you are ready to play football. Football is football. It's not just conditioning."

Celebrating the "miracle" Super Bowl triumph over Atlanta at City Hall. (photo by Stan Grossfeld)

REPETITION AND EXPERIENCE

"Seeing and reacting as quickly as you have to do it at this level in this league is a lot different than running sprints. You see 21 other guys moving and that means you have to do a certain thing, whatever your job is on that play. So seeing it, reacting to it, being able to get the jump on it and anticipate it—those are all the things that come with repetitions and experience."

YEAR-TO-YEAR IMPROVEMENT

"We've seen plenty of players that maybe haven't done a lot in Year 1, haven't done a lot in Year 2 and then Year 3 becomes a big year. As long as a player is improving and he's getting better, that's really the curve that you are looking for. You can't always identify when that time is going to come, but as they're cresting, sometimes it's in the middle of Year 1, it's the beginning of Year 2, it's the middle of Year 3. We can cite plenty of examples of players who had their big year in Year 3....

"Each situation is a little bit different. Sometimes it depends where the player came from, what his background was, what type of system he played in, what he was asked to do, how quickly he can learn to do the things he's being asked to do here. Some cases, that's very similar to what guys were asked to do in another program, techniques and things like that. In some cases it's very different.

"The level of competition can be a factor, too. What type of players he played against in college relative to the level of competition here. Just the whole schedule, the length of the season, the maturity, and so forth. There are so many variables that go in there, I'd have a hard time saying it's this one particular thing. But I think when you scout players and you bring them into your program you usually have an idea of where you think they are. Whether it turns out that way exactly you don't know until you spend time with them and have them in your program on a consistent basis. But you have a sense that some guys are probably going to be a little closer to being ready than others."

MEASURING INJURY RISK

"I wish I knew the answer to that question. If I did I'd be a lot better off. We see guys coming out of college that have never been hurt and they're hurt. We've seen guys coming out of college that had injuries in college and don't get hurt. We've seen guys that have played for a team and been injured and go somewhere else in free agency and never get injured and vice versa. I don't know.

Are some guys more prone than others? I mean, yes, but can you really quantify that? No. Some guys you think do everything they can. Every indicator you have says that they're as healthy as they're going to be. They have good flexibility, good strength, good balance. They have good everything and sometimes they end up [injured].

"You can't take out insurance, so you've just to go out there and play and whatever happens, happens. You can measure how players deal with injuries. I think you can measure that. Some guys deal with things differently than others do. But can you predict who's going to get a high-ankle [sprain], who's going to get a shoulder, who's going to break a bone? I don't know how you measure that. I wish I did."

AFTER MISSING TIME

"That is the question. How much is too much? How do you get ready for the speed of the game when you haven't been at the speed of the game? Anytime you bring an injured player back, sometimes the injury is part of that whole conversation. How much can he do? It could be other situations. What kind of condition is the player in based on the time that he has been away?… It's trying to find that sweet spot for getting the player the best preparation you can. My experience with all of those players has been, as time goes by they play better. Maybe their first game will be their best game but most likely the third, fourth, fifth, sixth games will probably be better than the first."

CHAPTER 3

Roster

FOR THE PATRIOTS, AS FOR OTHER NFL CLUBS, THEIR
53-man roster and 10-man practice squads are organic,
changing from week to week. Once the season starts, additions usually are made to replace injured players. But for
Bill Belichick and the front office the mission to improve
the team at every position is a year-round endeavor. "Every
player that's available, we consider," he said.

From Draft Day through training camp, when rivals
are reducing their numbers, until the trading deadline
and beyond, Belichick and the club's player personnel
staff routinely evaluate a dynamic pool of hundreds
of players.

"Every week we talk about personnel," said Belichick,
"and we go through the players that are on our roster, the
players that are on the practice squad, the players that

are available that are out on the street that aren't with any team, the players that are on other teams' practice squads, and anything that might have changed from the previous week."

More successfully than almost all of their opponents, the Patriots have managed over the years to build rosters for both the short and long term by knowing precisely what players they need and how to acquire them. "There's no magic formula for anything," Belichick observed. "It's a very inexact science, for sure."

OFF-SEASON EVALUATIONS

"We go through the same procedure every year in the off-season. We look at our team and look at the options we have to improve our team at every position. We don't narrow it down to anything. We don't exclude anything. Every player that's available, we consider. Some of them we tried to add to our team and were able to and some of them we've tried to add and we weren't. And that includes players that are on our team at the end of the season who are not on our team the following year.... Each year you try to build your team and make it as strong as you can. Whoever you think can help do that, you try to work it out with them. Sometimes you do, sometimes you don't."

ASSEMBLING A ROSTER

The NFL has a roster limit of 53 players, which requires coaches to use jigsaw-puzzle techniques to create two-deeps on offense and defense and also make room for special teamers. When Belichick and his staff are making decisions on the final few players, their versatility is paramount.

"You've got to have a team that can do the things you want it to in terms of personnel groupings and has some depth. You also have to be able to handle all the responsibilities in the kicking game, from gunners to inside-coverage people to wedge blockers to guys that can play on the wing in the punt team and all that. You look at a lot of people doing different things in training

Belichick formulating an answer after the third straight loss at the start of his inaugural 2000 season. (photo by Bill Greene)

camp to evaluate your depth and then when you come down to getting your roster you have to make sure that all those spots are covered. It's really a mosaic of all of that. It's not a third-down running back versus another third-down running back. It's all the things that come into play that those players would do or the other value that they would bring to your roster that if they do them then you don't need somebody else somewhere else to do them. Or if they don't do them then you do need somebody somewhere else or somehow you've got to get those things filled.

"It's a very inexact science. With 53 players, which is really only 45, you just can't have the depth that every coach would like to have. Some positions you have it, at other positions you don't. I don't think there's any way to ever have the kind of depth that all the NFL coaches would like to have on their roster. It's just not possible. So you pick and choose where you want to have it and the quality of it and then you go with it. If something happens then you make adjustments along the way."

RELEASING PLAYERS

While the NFL allows clubs to bring 90 players into training camp in mid-July, it also requires them to release more than three dozen of them by September 1 in order to reach the 53-man limit. The enforced exodus often makes for excruciating

decisions for the coaching staff and difficult conversations with
players who may never again wear a helmet.

"It's the worst part of the job. You start with 90 players and you know you're going to have to release 37 of them. It's usually more than that because other players come and are part of that process, too. Guys work hard, they give you everything they've got, they go out there and compete, and not everybody can make it. It's always a tough time of year for myself and all the other position coaches as well because those guys spend a lot of time with those players in meetings, watching film with them, out on the practice fields in smaller groups, and really try to develop a good working relationship with those players and it's hard to see it end.... It doesn't really get any easier. It's always a grouping of people and you're affecting their lives and their families and their careers and trying to do what's best for the team. But that can still be tough. It's tough."

LONG-TERM VS. SHORT-TERM NEEDS

"If you were just picking the team for one game, for the opener, that would be one thing. If you were picking the team strictly for next year, that would be another thing. But in reality you're trying to pick a team for all of those. You've got a game to play, you've got the early part

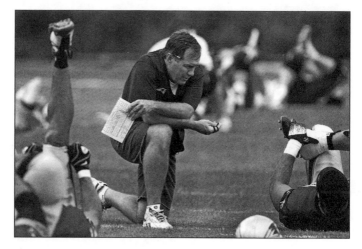

The coach observes stretching exercises during 2009 training camp. (photo by John Tlumacki)

of the season to be ready for. Sixteen games, that's a lot of football, and you need a lot of depth to get through those 16 games but you don't know exactly where you're going to need it.

"It's one big balancing act. You know you're going to have a team next year so do you want to keep a player this year, but you're really looking at where he's going to be next year? You don't think he's going to be a big contributor this year but you see that player has an upside to improve the following year. Or, do you go with a player who maybe has a little bit of a higher performance now but a year from now would somebody else pass him? Those are all tough questions....

"It's always hard to leave that veteran experience for a little bit of an unknown, but the lifeline of this league and the lifeline of every team is young developing players. You can't build a team without them, so they're an important part of it. There's uncertainty there. Not all of them develop. Then that, at the end, just becomes a waste of time. Just trying to make the right decisions there, especially when sometimes the information is limited. But it is what it is."

ACQUISITION TIMING

"Acquisitions that you make at the beginning of the season, in the spring or in the off-season, you're looking at roster building. You're looking at players that you feel would be competitive in a certain position or in a certain role or in a combination of roles that would be competitive for your team. That role might be as a starter, it might be as a rotational player, but whatever that is, you're looking for a guy that's going to be competitive in those roles.

"When you acquire a guy at the beginning of the season or in the season you're usually acquiring that player to fill a specific role at that time. He's not in competition with eight other guys for something. I mean, the reason you've acquired him is because he's available and it's worked out and you see a role for that player that you can use…. It's different than when you get a guy in March. Certainly you have a lot more time with that player, but your team's not really established at that point, either. You're still trying to see how it's all going to play out.

"In September or October, you have a lot better idea how it's playing out and if you acquire a player generally it's to put that player into a role that you feel is necessary and that he can do…. Other things happen, too. What you do at the end of September for one reason, by the middle of November those reasons may not be valid any more. You might be in a whole different ballgame and then maybe that player fits into that new situation or maybe he doesn't. Maybe somebody else fits into it. So you can't oversimplify it because each case is different."

POTENTIAL ADDITIONS

"Every time you bring a player on to your team I think you want to have an idea of what you're going to do with them, what you're going to ask them to do, and whether or not you feel like he can do it. Whether you draft them or sign them as a free agent or a veteran free agent or whatever the situation is, here's what you envision this guy's responsibilities being and what he needs to do. And then, whether or not you think he has the skill, the makeup and maybe in some cases experience, depending on what that role is, to do it.

"There's no magic formula for anything. It's a very inexact science, for sure, but you try to identify what you're looking for and then find people that fit that particular niche or role or criteria, however you want to look at it. If you feel like it will be productive, then you do it. If you don't, then you keep looking. Sometimes you find a guy that you think will and for whatever reason you don't get him. Somebody else drafts him or you're not able to sign him or whatever. And then maybe that opportunity comes up later on. Or maybe it doesn't. It's a regular process. It's very cyclical. We go through it many times during the year and then the next year we go through it again."

BEST PLAYER AVAILABLE

"At the start of the season you have your Best Player Available list, like Mel Kiper's. Here are the top five, six, seven guys, however many it is, that aren't on an NFL roster that you would like to spot if you have a need. And then there is another list of guys that are just the next player. Our next tackle, our next center, our next quarterback, our next receiver, our next whatever. But within that group there's just, who are the best football players? Forget about what our needs are. Who are the best players out there right now? Or who were they then and who are they right now?

"Even now [mid-October] you look at some of the players that are out there and there are three or four guys that I'm surprised they're not on NFL rosters and if we had an opportunity to put one of them on our roster it would be something we'd have to think about. But you get to this point in the season and it's hard to make moves at one position because you usually don't have enough depth at the position to do it. Usually it's more of a one-for-one swapout. We're swapping out this guy for another player at that position. But if you really feel that strongly about a player and his ability, then either you make room or, when you have room, then that's a player that gets a lot of consideration."

PLAYER POOL

"Every week we talk about personnel and we go through the players that are on our roster, the players that are on the practice squad, the players that are available that are out on the street that aren't with any team, the players that are on other teams' practice squads, and anything that might have changed from the previous week.

"For example, players that maybe were injured in preseason and they're getting healthier. Maybe they're not ready to play now so the team did an injury settlement with them, but they'll be ready in a couple of weeks or they'll be ready in a month. Other players that we have on what we call our short list. If we were to go to somebody if we needed a player and he gets signed by another team, who's the next player? What guys do we want to bring in for workouts based on, do we need a physical on them? Do we want to evaluate them? Is it a player we know? Maybe we don't need to work out a player that we know or have a lot of familiarity with, but maybe a guy we don't, a younger player or a guy that pops up somewhere along the line.

"You try to stay on top of the preseason games but in all honesty it's hard to watch a couple thousand players in preseason. So those first two, three, four weeks of the season you can really go back and take a closer look at the preseason games and zero in on a particular player that flashes at you. Then maybe you can go back and watch him in college and do more work on him. Those players might surface on a practice squad and things like that.

"It's a constant process with no 'We have to have this many guys in' or 'We have to have this many players on this list.' Sometimes you can have five emergency receivers and no emergency tackles or whatever it happens to be. Where does your next player come from? He can either come from your practice squad or he can come from a player that's not with a team or that's not practice-squad eligible. Unless you put him on your team you don't have him but he might be your next guy. We go through that every week."

Belichick posing with country singer Kenny Chesney during 2017 camp. (photo by John Tlumacki)

PERSONNEL DECISIONS

In a high-velocity contact sport, injuries are so frequent that the NFL has a nine-page policy on reporting them. Like all coaches, Belichick and his staff have to determine whom to put on the PUP list (Physically Unable to Perform) during the preseason (those players can return by Week 6 of the regular season) and whom to assign to injured reserve, which is a season-ending decision. More years than not, the number of Patriots on injured reserve is in double figures.

"All personnel decisions are difficult to make. There's not any player on our roster or our practice squad that we don't think is a good player or that we think has no future. If that's the way we felt about them then they wouldn't be here. So we feel like every player on the practice squad and certainly all 53 of the players that we have and even some of the other players—some players on PUP, some players that are on injured reserve—we feel like all of those players have a future and would have a role on the team, too. Could we keep one over another? I'm sure that all those have been discussed or debated at some point here, sometime along the way over the course of the last few months. So there're really no easy decisions with players like that.

"If any of them had clearly established themselves then we wouldn't be talking about it.... So the fact that they haven't, whether that's a situation where they're not ready or they're still developing or maybe they just didn't have the opportunity to do it yet and we just don't know until they get that opportunity. Those are decisions that you talk about and could go either way. There are a lot of different moving parts and a lot of factors that weigh into it and in the end you just have to try to decide what you think is the right thing to do. The more obvious it is, the easier the decision is. The less information, the less real hard data that you have to go on…until it's actual true performance, then there're more question marks."

TALKING WITH RIVALS

"You talk about personnel with teams all the time. It's fairly common. There's less of it now [mid-October] because teams are pretty well set but in the off-season and heading into the training camp period and during training camp when there is a lot of juggling of rosters going on, you talk to other teams about a lot of different personnel. And you talk to teams that would help you but don't want to help another team. Sometimes there is a flow of information there, too. It's not always about getting somebody. It's more of just knowing what is going on with that team and what's going on with certain players. It's more of an information flow. The actual 'I'll trade you this guy for that guy' thing, those are, I'd say, relatively few and far between. But the information flow on players is much greater than that."

CUTDOWN CONVERSATIONS

"There is no set formula. We talk about our players and what our needs are. What we want to try to do, who can do it. There are a lot of different points of view, from the position coaches to the coordinators to the special teams and so forth. Simultaneously, you have the personnel department, Nick Caserio [director of player personnel] and his staff, evaluating players on the other 31 teams as well as ours and making comparisons. Are there other players relative to the ones we have, some of which are available, most of which aren't? It becomes at some point a culmination of pulling all that information together and making a decision.

"Certainly there have been a lot of phone calls that come in and go out on various subjects and related personnel and decision-making and exchanges of players and so forth and so on. Sometimes it's on the run, sometimes its, 'Okay, we are going to meet at a certain time and go over it.' But sometimes things come up on the run and you have to take it as they come…. I'd say most of the calls relate more to exchanging information than, 'Here are seven players we want to trade; which six do you want to trade?' and then turn it into some big blockbuster trade."

ADDING DISCARDS

"We're not expecting teams to draft guys in the third round to release those players. So later draft choices and free agents, we identify those players on the other 31 rosters going into training camp. Here's four or five guys from each team that are based on the position, if they don't keep all of the players at that position then somebody is going to be out there, whether it's a player from the draft or maybe a veteran player. Who knows? So Nick Caserio and Dave Ziegler [pro personnel director] and pro personnel and scouts track those guys throughout the league. We monitor them and the guys that are available we follow up on. A lot of players that get released in the 53-cut that we might be interested in then re-sign with their team's practice squads and those players are never really available. Then there are other players that don't, for whatever reason, and we've worked out dozens of them…. Some of that is a function of the player. Some of it is a function of our situation. Some of it is a function of roster spot availability based on what our other practice squad needs are relative to depth and also relative to practice.

Sometimes there are guys out there that we would like to add to the practice squad. We just don't have room for them. Sometimes there are guys that we add to the practice squad that maybe we'd rather have another guy but we need the player at that position because of the practice needs. It's a little bit of a balance of that. When you can find a player that you want at a position that you want to add a guy to, then that's a pretty good fit."

EARLY-SEASON TRADING

"Historically you find that there's still a decent amount of roster movement in those first two or three weeks of the season. Just trying to strengthen your roster where you can, and then after that it's more a reaction to events or something that's happening on your team that you need to address to change. But I think those first two or three weeks there is still a pretty good opportunity to juggle things around to try to strengthen your roster and maybe address depth concerns that we probably all feel like we have when you make the final cut down to 53."

IN-SEASON TRADING

"To bring in a player now and teach him your system is tough because even if he learns it on paper or in a playbook and is actually going out there and doing it there are limited opportunities. So you trade for a guy and by the time you get him ready to go the season is over.

MID-SEASON TRADES

"Generally speaking it's hard to trade guys around the fifth, sixth game of the year because in football there is such a transition period. To bring somebody onto your team now and have to teach him a whole new system and then learn it and really be functional for you in the 10 regular season weeks that are left is asking a lot…. If it's a new guy coming onto your team at a third of the way through the season it's a lot different than bringing a new guy on at the end of August when you have the full 16 weeks to go. So it makes it a little bit harder. I think that's why you see less of it. I know baseball is a team sport and all that. I'm not saying that. But playing third base and playing left guard, there is a lot more integration that needs to be done on a football team, whatever position a guy plays, than what my sense of it is in baseball playing left field. I don't know how different left field is from one team to the next. I'm sure there's some differences but I don't think it's quite the same as what we go through."

PREPARING MID-SEASON PICKUPS

"Having them know what to do to be able to get out on the field is important. We've got to do a good job of teaching it, obviously condensing or streamlining information because you can't get the whole playbook in. And they've got to do a good job of working hard to learn it and specifically learn that game plan. So a lot of times you try to get them on the game plan first and then the next week you get the next game plan but maybe you can start to add some things to it and eventually over time be able to catch up on the overall nomenclature, terminology, more of a comprehensive understanding.

"And that varies from player to player, too—how experienced they are, how much experience they've had in a system similar to ours or things that they can relate to or where there is carryover. Every one is a little bit different. Each of us learns differently. Some things we pick up quicker than others, so it is individualized between that player and whichever staff members and his position coach are a part of that. Getting him up to speed, covering what he needs to know for that game, but also getting him acclimated into all the other aspects of our program, too. Not just the plays, but there are a lot of other things they need to learn or fall in line with."

LANGUAGE BARRIER

"If you get into a habit of saying certain words and those words now mean something different in our terminology then those are habits that have to be broken because they're just counterproductive. They mess us up because what they mean to the player they don't mean to anybody else…. It happens out there all the time where a certain formation or a certain play will happen and a guy will say something and we all look at him like, 'Who are you talking to, because we don't have that?' But to him it's something that he's learned and he's dealt with for a long time in his career and it means something to him. But that's just not a term that we use and they have to break that habit and get into using a term that means the same thing in our language."

DOWNSIDE OF MID-SEASON TRADES

"You bring in a player this late in the year that doesn't know your system and hasn't been with you. At this point in time we've had over half the practices for the entire year that have already occurred because of the number we have in training camp and in preseason. To bring in a player now and teach him your system is tough because even if he learns it on paper or in a playbook and is actually going out there and doing it there are limited opportunities. So you trade for a guy and by the time you get him ready to go the season is over."

Belichick brandishes the Super Bowl trophy after the astounding comeback against the Falcons in Houston. (photo by Barry Chin)

TRADING DEADLINE

"You need more, there's less available, it's a shorter season. You're trading for a guy for just a short amount of time. How quickly can you get him ready, how productive will it be, was it really worth it? Is it worth it to the team who is trading away the player to get not very much for somebody versus just keeping him and playing with him even though you get something for him but it isn't really worth it? You'd rather have him for those seven, eight games, whatever is left, than some pick at the end of the draft that you might not think has a lot of value, especially if you're worried about your depth at that position with the player that you're moving.

"Usually when you have that kind of depth you see more of those trades in September when the value is higher and teams have more depth at that position so it's easier for them to move the player because they have other guys at that point. But two months later they have less depth at that position and they're less likely to move them. That's just one man's opinion. It's not a survey of the league or anything. It's hard to get a guy ready in a short amount of time. I don't know much about baseball but maybe a third baseman on this team, put him at third base on the other team and let him hit. How much is there involved? I'm sure there's some but it's not like playing left guard, having 20 different protections and two dozen running plays and a dozen different defenses you have to block every week. It's a little more involved."

PRACTICE SQUAD PHILOSOPHY

The NFL allows clubs to keep 10 practice players on hand to fill in for injuries and the Patriots usually are at the limit. While those players are guaranteed a minimum of $7,600 a week, the more valuable ones can make significantly more. Many practice players either have been or will be on a regular season roster and can be signed by another club, who must immediately give them a jersey number.

"We've had players that when we look at our practice squad we would say, 'Okay, these players could be activated, they're our next guy. If something were to happen here, if something were to happen there, that would be our next guy.' There are other situations where if something were to happen at that position that practice squad player probably wouldn't be the next player. It would be somebody else that's not on your roster and it could be for a couple different reasons. One is the player's development—we think he's going to develop into a player but he's just not ready now.

Other players have more versatility and can do different things for you and they can practice in two or three positions and help the other players get ready but we don't feel they are quite at the developmental level to be regular roster players. As the player improves, sometimes that changes. Maybe you don't think he's going to be and then he is, and we've certainly had players like that…. Players improve. Hard work, technique, physical development, and all those kinds of things.

"There's a lot of room to develop and we certainly can recite a lot of offensive linemen that fall into that category. We can also recite a lot of them that are on the practice squad that never played in the NFL. If you really feel like the player is a player and you don't want anyone else to have a shot at him you try to find a way to keep him on your roster. And if you're kind of not sure, then that's probably why they're on the practice squad."

PRACTICE SQUAD MAKEUP

"Your practice squad players give you depth on your roster so you can theoretically bring them up and put them on your roster. So there are eight [now 10] guys right there, depending on what position they play or what they do, that could help you in one way or another potentially. But 10 guys aren't enough to support a whole football team. We don't have a kicker on the practice squad. There are a lot of things we don't have on the practice squad that if we needed one, we'd have to get one somewhere else unless you had some way to handle it on your team....

"Every week there are things that have changed on your team. There are things that have changed with what's available on the street. There are other players that have been released from other teams or guys that have been dropped off their practice squads. There's a constant turnover there, I'd say until probably about halfway through the season. Then everybody is pretty much settled into where they're at. Normally at that point teams are losing players and they have to bring a replacement in. Whereas now [late September] there's turnover that's occurring where teams are trying to upgrade their personnel or find better combinations."

PRACTICE SQUAD PROTOCOLS

"Say a team signs a player from another practice squad. You have to keep that player on your roster for three weeks, as opposed to signing a player that's not with a team who you can bring on and take him off.... Say you have a spot and you bring on a guy from another team's practice squad, put him on your team, and then you get an injury that week. Now you have to bring in somebody else to help you at that spot but you don't have the flexibility of

dropping the guy that you brought in the week before....
So when you sign somebody off a practice squad there's
an opportunity cost to it. I'm not saying it's not worth it,
but I'm just saying that's the cost to it. You have the player,
but you have the player. You can't do anything with him,
either, so that limits your options if something else were
to come up."

INCREASED VALUE OF PRACTICE SQUADDERS

"The further you get into the season, the more attrac-
tive your practice squad players are because they've been
with you longer, they know a little bit more, and you've
seen them out there on a daily basis versus somebody else
who, let's say, was released at the beginning of the season
and now we're in the 13th week and maybe the player
hasn't played in three months. Well, how long is it going
to take to get him up to speed versus how long is it going
to take for your practice squad player?

"He can kind of jump in there, he knows what to
do. Maybe he doesn't have as much experience or he's
a younger player but that's the trade-off. He's more cur-
rent than guys that were out of football now for a while.
That's less of an issue earlier in the year. You get in the
second, third, fourth week of the season and you bring
in a player that was just at training camp and preseason

games a couple of weeks ago. That's a little bit different than doing it now.

"When you look across the league, you look at the waiver wire on a Tuesday or Wednesday in December, that's just about what you're going to see. You're going to see 10, 11 guys going on injured reserve. And you're going to see 15 guys released, maybe 10 of them go on injured reserve and five of them are releases. And then probably 10 of those replacements are going to be from the team's practice squad and then five of them will come from somewhere else—a team changed kickers, or something like that—and you find those players. With each week it's going to be the same."

TEAM CHEMISTRY

"Every team is different. Every team has a different makeup and a different chemistry and sometimes it changes over the course of the year based on the circumstances that a team goes through. I don't think there's any right or wrong, it has to be this or it has to be that. You put any group of people together and you're going to have a different chemistry, and if you change a few people then that will change and the circumstances that group goes through will force some changes. It just will. It's inevitable. The most important thing is the execution and

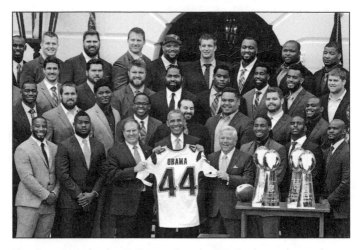

The Patriots make the 44th president their 54th player during the White House visit following the Super Bowl victory over the Seahawks. (photo by John Tlumacki)

the consistency of the units in the overall team. Emotion is great and that can be a big part of it but in the end we can't all sit around and kumbaya all day. If you don't block anybody or you can't tackle or you can't kick then I don't really know what you have. I'm not saying it's not important. It's part of it, but you better be able to execute what you're doing at a pretty high level or I don't think the rest of it is going to carry you all that far."

CHAPTER 4

Training Camp

WHETHER OR NOT THE PATRIOTS WIN THE SUPER BOWL, the following season begins at the bottom of the mountain with a refashioned roster and a renewed challenge. "It's a constant race for 16 weeks to get your football team better and better and better and better, but they're doing that on the other side, too," Bill Belichick mused. "When the season starts, as much as anybody wants to say, 'Well, we'll start off where we were last year,' there's no way. There's no way."

A substantial amount of training and tutelage needs to be accomplished in eight weeks of preseason camp and exhibition games. "It's like building a house," the coach observed. "You cut some corners and then you don't have the walls put up properly and then the sheetrock doesn't go on right and then you have to go back and fix it up and

The coach surveys his domain during the 2016 training camp. (photo by John Tlumacki)

everything. That's not the way to do it. You want to get it in right but at the same time we're on a time schedule, too. We don't have forever."

As a guide, Belichick and his staff will consult their camp notes from previous seasons. "We will go back and evaluate what we did, how we did it, what things were good, what things we would like to do differently, suggestions for next year, problems we had," he said, "and try to be on the front end of those the next time around."

BACK TO BEGINNINGS

"You get to the end of the year and then you start the next year and you think, 'Okay, where are we? Well, we're nowhere close to where we were in December or January. We're just not. We're starting training camp, we have new people, nobody has run these plays in six months.' It takes you a period of time. Even if you have some spring practices, still you're just nowhere near the execution level.... I'm not saying we're great in December. We're better in December—well, so is everybody else. From an execution standpoint, what we can do now and what we can do in September are two different things. A big part of it is just the newness and the getting back to the timing and the execution of your basic plays and then adjustments and situations and all those kinds of things. That's the way I see it.

"Now, you can look at the stats like I'm sure everybody does and say, 'Look at how great the Patriots were in September.' That's only relative to where anybody else was in September. It's not relative to where you are. We're better now than we were in September, there's no question about that. Even though maybe you don't want to believe that but I know we are. But where is everybody else? And if they've improved more than we have, then the results are a little different. Or if we have improved more than they have, the results could be a little bit different. It's a constant race for 16 weeks to get your football team better and better and better and better, but they're doing that on the other side, too. When the season starts, as much as anybody wants to say, 'Well, we'll start off where we were last year,' there's no way. There's no way. It takes so long to build to that point that you have to be realistic. You just can't do the things that you did a year ago in December, in September."

CAMP PROGRESS

From the moment that camp opens in mid-July until the regular season commences on the Thursday after Labor Day, the countdown clock is ticking for Belichick and his staff to instruct, evaluate, and whittle down their 90 candidates to 53. Since league rules limit the number of padded practices and hours on the field, the traditional four exhibition games are invaluable in helping the coaches decide which players are ready for prime time.

"There are certain things that you have to get done, certain situations you have to cover and things like that. We just take it day to day, and things that aren't looking as good we spend more time on and try to correct them or maybe even throw them out. Sometimes we adjust what we do and put in something new or build on something that we feel like is going better and can be a strong point for us. I don't think you could sit there at the beginning of training camp and say, 'Well, this is exactly where we're going to be in September.' There are a lot of variables between the time you start training camp and the time you open the season. Along the way you're just trying to do the best thing that you can for the team and everybody involved. Players are at different stages of their preparation. Some guys have never played before. Some guys have played a lot. Some guys have worked together with each other before, some guys haven't. There are just so many variables. I think you just try to do what is best for your team and do that on a day-to-day basis."

PLAY RETENTION

While the physical demands of an NFL training camp are daunting, especially for rookies adjusting to the size, speed, and savvy of professional football players, the more challenging aspect for Patriots players is mental. The playbook can contain as many as 1,000 pass plays alone, reckons quarterback Tom Brady, who expects his receivers to know them all.

"What coaching is in training camp is trying to give the players the right amount of information. You don't want to not move ahead but at the same time you don't want to move ahead too quickly, where you then have to go back and do it all over again. It's like building a house. You cut some corners and then you don't have the walls put up properly and then the sheetrock doesn't go on right and then you have to go back and fix it up and everything. That's not the way to do it.

"You want to get it in right but at the same time we're on a time schedule, too. We don't have forever. We have a preseason game in two weeks and [then] we open the season, so we have a schedule where we have to have everything ready by then to some degree. You try to manage those two things but at the same time everybody on your team isn't at the same place. You have some players who are much more experienced and are further ahead than others so you try to find that balance and that's really what coaching is.

"Sometimes some groups can move faster than others on your team and so as a head coach and as a coordinator you have to talk about those things and try to figure out what the best thing is for the team. And that might not be the best thing for each individual player but that's what football is. It's a team sport and we all have to give up some individual preferences when we sign up for the team. That's part of it, too."

DEVELOPING VERSATILITY

"At some point in camp we'll probably move just about every player either from one position to another or just switch sides in the same position to give ourselves depth and versatility. I think everybody should be expecting that at one point or another, with a couple of exceptions. For the most part, everybody will have some degree of learning multiple positions and building some versatility, both for themselves and for the team."

Belichick amid the quickened pace of a joint practice with the Jaguars in 2017. (photo by John Tlumacki)

CONDITIONING

"Every play that players play in preseason is beneficial from a learning standpoint, a technique standpoint, and also conditioning. We run around the field and all of that and that's great for conditioning but it's still not quite the same as actually playing the game and the intensity of it. What actually occurs in the game and the conditioning levels that a player has to be in to play a game, we try to simulate those in practice but it isn't quite the same. Whichever players play, when they're in there they get those opportunities and experiences and when they don't, then it goes to some other players."

VALUE OF SCRIMMAGES VS. PRACTICES

"Instead of doing one thing for a sustained period of time, which isn't really the way football is played, this gives us a chance to simulate the moving game. First down, second down, third down, ball moves, field position moves, the kicking unit comes on the field, other offensive or defensive unit comes out on the exchange. That's how you play. You don't run 10 first-down plays in a row. You don't run eight third-down plays in a row or eight sub-blitzes in a row or 10 punts in a row. That's just not football, but those are good teaching methods and it's a more efficient way to do it, so there's a place for that. But at some point there's a place for trying to simulate a game, so that's what we're going to do."

JOINT PRACTICES

After having one joint practice in 2001 with the Giants, his former club, Belichick didn't schedule another for nine years. The Patriots routinely have had two of them during each preseason and penciled in three in 2017 with the Texans, Lions, and Jaguars, whom they ended up facing both in the exhibition opener and in the AFC Championship Game. This year the Patriots scheduled no joint sessions.

"We have a certain practice structure, a certain way of doing things. It's not right or wrong, it's just the way we do them. You have another team that, they're playing the same game but maybe they do things just a little bit differently. When those don't coincide, then as coaches we try to find what the common ground is. Either we're going to do it your way or you're going to do it our way or we're going to split the difference, depending on what the issue is. I wouldn't say that's challenging but that's one of the things that needs to be ironed out.

"It's usually better if everybody can do it the same way, so there are certain periods at the beginning of practice where both teams do their own thing separately and then when we come together there's a certain standard or conformity that we want there to be so that everybody's on the same page. It's not one way for our defense and another way for their defense…. In general, that's how it goes. Once you have the conversation with the coach and we agree, 'Well, this is conceptually the way we want to do it,' then it's dotting the i's and crossing some t's and just working it out so that we can actually get to the point that we agree on."

CAMP NOTES

"I look at the last two or three years of notes from before training camp, and during training camp and then after training camp when we talk about what happened.

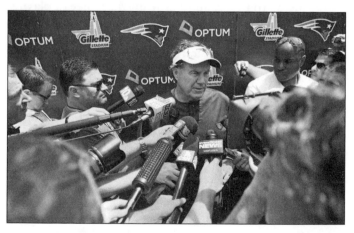

During training camp Belichick may chat with his questioners al fresco, as he did here in 2015. (photo by Jonathan Wiggs)

We will go back and evaluate what we did, how we did it, what things were good, what things we would like to do differently, suggestions for next year, problems we had—and try to be on the front end of those the next time around. There is definitely an element of looking back at previous years and trying to take the best things from those camps that we felt like we did as a team and incorporating those in the future at camps, and also trying to eliminate the problems or address them sooner, rather than after they become an issue."

DIFFERENCE BETWEEN PRESEASON AND REGULAR SEASON

"Other teams have much better scouting reports on our players, as we do on theirs. By the time you get to the regular season and you've seen guys play in preseason or a couple of regular season games, you can start to identify their strengths and weaknesses and they can start to identify ours. The game planning is different, the way that your matchups are. Players try to play to your weakness and avoid your strength. That's something you don't always see in the first two or three preseason games because nobody really cares that much about it. That's a big thing now, the situational football, getting to know the other teams, their personnel, their tendencies, their coordinators. How they do things, how much it changes from week to week, not just out there running around. It's very specific.

"It's a huge transition from the preseason to the regular season and I'd say it's a huge transition within the regular season. The games are a lot different than they're going to be three, four, five weeks from now when there's a lot more evidence in the books. Then teams start dealing with injuries and replacements and adjustments and everybody is adding to their scheme. Each week you add a couple new plays, a couple new looks, you add a wrinkle, those kind of things. What looks like a tendency is really just bait for something that they're going to try to set up and show you something they've been doing and something else off it. All those are learning experiences and it's a much higher level than what you see in college football, particularly in the passing game [that's the big difference] and the kicking game."

CHAPTER 5

Season

WHAT TRADITIONALLY SETS THE PATRIOTS APART FROM the rest of the league is their progressive improvement from summer to winter. Under Bill Belichick's direction, the team has compiled a 64–13 record in December, the best in NFL history.

"We try to take pride in our performance every week, from Game 1 to Game whatever," the coach said. "That's the way we do it. Come in, prepare for the team, get ready to go, try to play our best on Sunday, and try to win. That's what we do every week."

The essence of the Patriots' philosophy is consistent and efficient preparation with prime emphasis on what each player's contribution needs to be for the team's success. "This is what your role is," Belichick and his staff tell them. "This is what your job is. First things first."

As the week progresses, the coaches distill and prioritize the details that they believe will make the difference between defeat and victory. "What are the most important things that we have to do here to win?" Belichick asks his players. "We know there are 1,000 things we've talked about and everything is important, but in the end, let's get back to what we need to do here tomorrow."

While the stakes undeniably are higher in December than they are in September, the Patriots' approach is undeviating. "We try to play good football all year long," said Belichick. "We try to coach well. We don't always do it, but we're trying."

STEADY IMPROVEMENT

"Early in the year everything is so new and fresh. You start playing games and nobody has played a full game in preseason. You build up your stamina and you build up your routine, which is different than what it is in training camp as far as your weekly preparation. You start to expand your playbook a little bit, and your opponents, each week you see a little bit more from each of them progressively. It's important that we keep working to improve as a football team and individually.

"Fundamentally, here are the things we need to do better, these types of plays or your individual techniques,

Belichick pleading for reconsideration from the officials amid a resounding 2002 loss at Tennessee. (photo by Matthew Lee)

things like that. I really make it a point to talk to a number of players individually on a weekly basis about, 'Look, this is what you need to do better,' or 'Here are some examples of plays over the last few weeks that [are] a problem, we have to get this.' 'Here's how you can do a better job,' or 'This is how we're going to do this differently.'

"I don't think it's so much of looking ahead as it is, there's a body of work here, there are a lot of games. Looking back at the last three, four, five, six games, what things can we do better than what we've been doing? There is certainly enough to go on, whereas those first few weeks, a lot of it is just trying to move forward with your team, but now we're seeing some of the same things every week. Teams are trying to do similar things to us, whether it's a weakness or scheme thing, whatever it is, we have to try to address it and take better care of it."

PRACTICE VS. GAME

"Practice is practice. It's the closest we can get to simulating a game. It's not game conditions, but it's as close as we can get. Players that can perform in practice I think have a chance to perform in the game. It's still another level, it's another step. But if you can't do it consistently in practice then it's pretty unlikely it's going to happen consistently in a game. That's true of every position on the field. I can't think of one that wouldn't fall into that category. You do what you can do. You make it as realistic as you can, or in some cases maybe you make it a little bit harder where you can in some areas and then the game is the game. It's a different speed. It's a different level."

COMPETITIVE PRACTICE LEVELS

"There are some drills that are as competitive as we can make them. There are other drills that are competitive to a point. Obviously we don't want a defensive back blowing up a receiver to break up a pass and things like that. Then there are other drills that aren't that competitive. We're trying to provide a look and we're trying to not make it a physical type of competition but more of a repetition/ execution type of drill. The most important thing is that everybody is practicing at the same tempo. You don't have one guy playing at one level and another guy playing at another level. We're all playing at the same level, whatever that is. I think those are your most productive practices.

"We have drills like one-on-one pass rush or one-on-one coverage or drills like that that are as competitive as you make them. You're out there trying to beat the other guy, he's trying to beat you. Then there are other drills that are tempo a little bit below that. It's competitive to a certain point. Then there are other drills that are really not intended to be competitive. They're intended more to be teaching and identification, recognition and execution, rather than the competition part of it. Based on what we're doing, what the drill is, what day of the week it is, what point in the season it is, what point in training camp—it could be any combination of those."

PRACTICING BAD SNAPS

"We do bad-snap drills with the holder and the punter, absolutely. That's always part of the mental preparation every week. Just to go through those and have the drill where the ball is high, low, on the ground, wobbly, wet-ball drills. We do those periodically."

CONTACT IN PRACTICE

Where NFL rules once had no limits on contact in practice, the league now restricts padded sessions to one per day in training camp and a total of 14 during the regular season, 11 of which must be held during the first 11 weeks. That poses a challenge to coaches to prepare players for games in which every play produces collisions.

"Practice is just preparation. It's a necessary part of getting ready for the game. It's not punishment. It's preparation. Whatever you can do to get your team prepared, whatever a player can do to prepare to play. Full-speed contact on every single play, every day of the week, at some point it is diminishing returns. It's counterproductive. I don't think anybody is in favor of that. But it's preparation, so you do the best you can as a coach to prepare your team. You do the best you can as a player to prepare yourself or prepare the teammates if you're working with them and you're giving them a look at what they're doing. You're the scout team, then you're helping them prepare, just like they help you prepare. That's the way I see all of that. It's about preparation. That's what practice is."

The coach signaling his players to decline a penalty during a 2015 rout of the Dolphins. (photo by Jim Davis)

BRINGING ALONG YOUNG PLAYERS

"Each week there's something that's a little bit new in preparing for the opponent, that's a little bit different from last week or a little bit different than something we've done. We're not trying to reinvent the defensive system but you add a call or you add an adjustment or you do something to take care of a problem that they're giving you. Whether they're giving you a lot of it or maybe they're not giving you that much of it but when it comes up, here's how you want to handle it. Those accumulate through the year and for young players that's part of the process.

"It's not just learning the stuff at training camp but learning the adjustments and the additions throughout the year. Some of those you might come back to when that situation from earlier in the season presents itself again. You might come back to that, so that experience is good for them. So do we keep doing more? Yeah, we do, because we have to defend more. To be honest with you, we have to defend more from the offense. You look at any team in the league after seven, eight, nine games, and they're doing more than they were doing in Week 2 and we're doing more than we were doing. The multiples add up."

LATE-SEASON PRACTICES

"We've taken a lot of snaps when you go all the way back to OTAs and training camp and all of the practices and all of the meetings. Do we need another snap at Ride 34 Bob? I don't know. We could always use it but we've had a lot of them this year. Do we need another snap at a coverage? You try to balance that out. How many more plays versus how much rest, walkthroughs versus practice, pads versus no pads, all of those things. But the more snaps you have, the further along you are. I would say in particular if you're doing something well then the more confidence you'd have that you'd be able to execute it at a good level. But you can't stop doing it. I don't think just sitting on a couch for a week is the way to get ready for a game. Even though you'd be well-rested, you'd leave a lot of other preparation components behind. So there's some kind of balance in there.

"Maybe you want a certain amount of rest but you have a certain amount of preparation to do, so where do you draw the line—60/40, 55/45, 70/30, 30/70? You have to make that decision. One thing that comes with having a long week that comes with a short week, to a certain degree you try to either get ahead or maybe get a little more rest in a long week knowing that you have a short week coming up or get further ahead so you don't have as much to do as you would normally have because you try to push some of it to where you have a little bit more time. Time management and efficiency, combining rest with your work product, it's all part of it."

MISSING PRACTICE

For NFL clubs, which only play 16 regular season games, practice days are precious. Since the players get one day off, since only one day in pads is permitted, and since Saturdays are limited to walkthroughs, Belichick and his assistants must make the most of every hour of on-field preparation.

"You still need to practice, you still need timing, you still need to see the plays develop on film. But can everyone take part in all of them? No. But can those guys still go out there and be effective and play? Yeah, I think they can. Is it better for them to practice? I'm sure it is. If everybody's 100 percent healthy they'd all be out there practicing and that would be better, that would be ideal, but it's not always [possible]. But I don't think that means it can't be functional.... Whoever isn't practicing, somebody else is in there for them.

"You don't want any player to miss practice, but in the long run it's a good thing for a player who doesn't get to play as much to be able to run our plays instead of just running the scout team plays. Whether that's your eighth or ninth offensive linemen that are sometimes inactive, whether it's your backup quarterback, whether it's some of the guys that don't get a lot of playing time at their positions. If they get a chance to play then it keeps them sharp doing our things rather than always running the other team's plays. So it's no different than training camp. If one guy's out that's an opportunity for somebody else to get better. When somebody comes back, that just gives us more depth and more people that can participate.

Belichick venting his disbelief and displeasure to the back judge in 2017's home loss to Carolina. (photo by Jim Davis)

Whatever you have you take advantage of it and make the most of it and make it a positive. Whatever the situation is, you make a positive out of it."

INJURED PLAYERS RESUMING PRACTICE

"You have to consider, depending on how long the player has been out, which practice you want to start him back on. Do you want to start him back on a Wednesday, which is a lot of times our most competitive practice with the most contact and the highest speed and the highest tempo? Or if you do it on a Friday then you're starting him at maybe a little bit lower tempo and see how that goes. Then maybe the practice on the following Wednesday the player has a little more confidence. At least he's been out there, he's done it. It's been at a little bit lower tempo or speed but at least he's been doing football drills.

"We can go out there, run in the bubble and do jumping jacks and do sit-ups and run up and down the field, but it's not the same as reading and reacting and performing your skills as a football player. So going out there and practicing is really the first chance that we get to see that, especially for a player that's been out. If it's a guy who played Sunday, didn't practice Wednesday, practices Thursday, then that's a different story. But a guy who's been out two, three, four, five weeks, whatever it is, he needs that time of playing football, not just running through the ropes and hitting a couple bags. You've got to have the other 21 guys out there, too.

"Each case is different. Sometimes you put a player back out there Wednesday. Sometimes you put him back out there Thursday. Sometimes it's Friday. Sometimes it has to do with his progression. Somctimes it's the tempo. Sometimes it's other circumstances that come into play so there's no set 'It's always this way.' It's A) when the player's ready, and B) once he's cleared medically to do it then it becomes a coaching decision as to when to do it or how to do it. Maybe you put him out there on Wednesday and you just let him do scout."

GAUGING INJURED PLAYERS' READINESS

"You can see more in practice than you can see in a walkthrough but practice isn't game speed. It's the best we have and you go by what you see. Over time, through experience and watching players and watching different tempos in practice, you get a gauge for it—and it's nothing specific. I don't even know if I could sit here and tell you exactly what it is, but I think you look at it and sometimes you say, 'Nope, I just don't think it's there.' And other times you say, 'Yeah, I think it is.' And sometimes you come off the field on Friday and say, 'I don't really think he can do it.' But then on Sunday you go out there and work out before the game and it looks different. And those 48 hours, or close to 48 hours, make a difference and things change. So that happens, too.

"Every situation's different and there's no set formula for making decisions. At least I don't have one.... It's inexact. We only play at game speed once a week, and then we

The coaching whistle at the ready during a playoff practice during the 2005 season. (photo by Jonathan Wiggs)

have a lot of practice opportunities during the course of the week on Wednesday, Thursday, Friday, or sometimes more than that in training camp and preseason. You just go by what you see. You talk to the position coach, you talk to the strength coach, you talk to the player, and with that whole composite you come up with some kind of decision. Maybe you put him out there on Wednesday and you just let him do scout team stuff and if that goes okay then you let him take his offensive or defensive reps on Thursday. There're 100 different scenarios."

INJURED PLAYER AVAILABILITY

"If a player has an injury, you rehab the injury until the injury is at a point where he can begin activity. Once he begins activity and there are no setbacks then you increase the level of activity until the player is ready to participate in mainstream with the rest of the team. Once he is ready to do that and he has demonstrated, [through] all the steps along the way, that he is ready to do that, then you put him into those situations, whether it's on a limited or full basis…. It doesn't matter if it's a wrist, an elbow, a shoulder, a knee. It's the same process and you just take those different steps along the way.

"Sometimes it goes like that. Sometimes it dips. Sometimes it levels off. It's very unpredictable, just like all of us when we don't feel good. We want to feel better and sometimes you feel better the next day and sometimes it takes two days. Sometimes it's a week. Sometimes it's two weeks. The next time you get a cold, we should say, 'When is this player going to be ready? When's he going to feel good? When's he going to be right?' Next time you get sick, you tell me the exact day that you're going to feel good and we'll make sure that you are confident and positive you can hit that target. It's impossible. You just take it day to day. What else can you do?"

DETERMINING ACTIVE PLAYERS

Though NFL teams carry 53 players on their rosters, only 46 are eligible to play in each game. Clubs must announce their seven inactive players 90 minutes before kickoff. The time when Belichick and his staff make their decision fluctuates from week to week.

"It varies. Sometimes you know on Friday that the player is just not going to be ready. All the indications are there. But there are other times that you truly don't know. If they're definitely not going to play then we list them as 'out' on the injury list. Or if we think it's really a long, long, long shot then we list them as 'doubtful.' If we don't know, then we list them as 'questionable.' In the next 48 hours between now and kickoff on Sunday, that's when that question mark gets answered. Sometimes they play, sometimes they don't. Or sometimes they can play but we elect not to play them for whatever the reasons are. Sometimes they just physically can't play. It could be any of the above."

INJURED PLAYERS' INPUT

"The players want to play. So not very often is a player going to tell you, 'I don't want to play.' Usually it's more along the lines of, 'I want to play, I can do these things.' Sometimes they tell you, 'I can't do these other things.' Sometimes you have to figure that out for yourself. Because a player wants to play, he won't mention, 'I don't really feel confident cutting to my left—I can play, I'll be all right.' My job is to do what I feel is best for the team and try to figure out if what he can do is good enough or if we're going to be able to accept that for the good of the team. Not that he won't give us his best—just, what is [his best]?"

EMERGENCY BACKUPS

"It could depend on what the game plan is or what the role is. Sometimes when you put a player into that position you realize that you're not going to ask him to do everything that you ask the player that normally plays the position to do. So if we have to make this personnel move then we'll be limited in these certain ways and here's how we'll work around that. Or maybe we don't work around that. It depends on what it is. But that comes up somewhere in every game. It's one thing to sit here and talk about it on Friday. It's another thing to talk about it Sunday afternoon at two o'clock when somebody's out and now it's an unanticipated move. Then it's, 'Okay, here's the next person we'd put in.' But what if something happens after that?

Belichick scrutinizes the action during the 2016 victory at Buffalo that avenged the earlier home loss. (photo by Barry Chin)

"I would say the higher degree of difficulty comes in the situational defenses depending on what your depth is, things like goal-line or dime or sub-defense. You have 66 spots on special teams, right? Eleven in six different units, so that's 66 players. You can't have 66 backups, so you've got to have one guy that might back up four or five things. If something happens to somebody then that one person gets plugged in. Then once you have that second injury it's a real scramble.

"Sometimes it affects your game plan, and sometimes you put the player in and you can run your game plan but sometimes you're limited in what you can do. For example, if you put an offensive lineman in for a tight end you'd have to change some things in the passing game. Maybe in protection, maybe not in the running game, possibly, or vice versa. If you put another receiver in the game maybe you can run the same passes but you lose that blocker if it was a tight end. You just have to work around that."

SENSING A GOOD WEEK OF PREPARATION

"You see the team is alert on different situations. They see things. They know what we want to do against it. They get it executed and then it comes up in the game and you're able to do it. Or you get something a little bit different and they're alert and they make the adjustment to it. 'That's sort of like what we practiced, but not quite.' Here's something that's a little bit different and they're able to make that adjustment, whether it's individually or collectively, two or three guys having to see it and adjust to it.

"Those are good signs, when you go out there to practice and the things you talked about in meetings, the things you walked through, the things you've shown on film, when you present them… they handle it properly. If it's a little bit different, not quite the way you talked about it, they're able to make those adjustments and sort it out. So if you see that on Sunday some of those situations come up and if you're able to handle those as a carryover of what you've seen during the week of practice and preparation, that's a good sign."

PRIORITIZING INSTRUCTIONS

"You always want to prioritize what's important because by the end of the week we're sitting here on Friday or Saturday and every player has been told 1,000 things. 'Do this. Do that. When this happens, do this. When that happens, do that. If they do this, you're going to check to that. Read this guy. Read that guy.' He's got 1,000 things in his mind and I think it's important to boil it back down to, 'Okay, those are all techniques and they're all adjustments and they're things we need to do but what do we need to do to win this game? Let's make sure we've got first things first.'

"Because somewhere between those 1,000 things there's one and then there's 1,000. There's got to be some kind of priority. So every time you come to the end of the week you want to bring it back to what are the most important things to do as a team and at each position: Here are the three most important things for you to do this week. So that you don't lose sight of the big picture and so you don't take a chance on players not knowing what the most important things are and making those decisions themselves. You remind them that this is how the game is played. This is what your role is. This is what your job is. First things first."

CHANGING GAME PLANS

"That happens pretty much every week. Sometimes it's on Thursday, sometimes it's on Friday, sometimes it could even be on Saturday. We could say, 'Look, cross this play off. Cross that play off. Cross this adjustment off. We're not going to do that.' Either we ran it a couple times and for whatever reason—either it didn't look good or we didn't get a run right or we just don't have enough time to practice it against what we really think we're going to see. We just say, 'That's it.' And we talk to the players about that, too. Particularly the quarterback, but not just the quarterback. If we had a secondary or the linebackers and we talked to them at the end of the week and they're like, 'I still don't feel really good about this,' well all right. You know what? We don't need it. We've got other stuff we can call, hopefully. The whole game isn't just hinged on this one thing. If Tom [Brady] says, 'You know what? I don't really feel good about this play down here, they do this, they do that.' Okay, well, maybe if you ran it three or four more times—but we don't have time to run it three or four more times.

"So you just say, 'Okay, let's pull the plug on it. We have other plays. We have other stuff we feel good about, so let's forget about that one.' We do a walkthrough on Saturday, but Friday is the last day where you really run everything. If something comes up today that's still a little bit dirty then that's probably not a good sign. But sometimes you have to do it and you say, 'Okay, look, we'll take a little more time on Saturday and set it up in the walkthrough. We've got to get this. When this happens, this is the only way we can handle it, so let's go through it one more time and make sure everybody's on the same page.'

"You get later in the week and you deal with some one-time situations—two-minute, backed-up, four-minute, two-point plays—that may or may not happen. Kickoff return after a safety—you know, all that stuff. You do it and if you make a mistake on it you've just to correct it and move on. You throw that out and then you've got to put something else in. The big thing is you want everybody to feel confident and feel good going into the game that what we're going to call we know what to do and we can be aggressive doing it. If you have that, then you've got a chance. If you don't and you can't play aggressively, then that's not what you want to do."

DAY BEFORE A GAME

"It's a review of everything that we're going to do. There are some situations the day before the game that we go over in the meetings or go over on the field in a walkthrough that we haven't covered prior to that week. You can't cover every situation in every game that could possibly come up. That would be impossible. But usually over the course of three to four weeks you can pretty much get them all. Maybe you kick off after a safety, kickoff return after a safety, the squib kick situations, the take-a-safety-on-a-punt, all those kinds of things.

"Just as an example, in the kicking game you maybe wouldn't cover every one of those every week but you cover two or three of them this week and then two or three of them the next week and then two or three of them, so then after a cycle of four to five weeks you would have hit it. Those things don't come up every single game. You're lucky if it's once a season. But any really critical plays, like a must onside kick or having to block a punt rush at the end of the game when you've got to punt the ball and you know they're coming—things like that are covered on a more weekly basis.

"And then we try to pull it all together so over the course of the week the players get told about 5,000

The coach with owner Bob Kraft, who hired him in 2000 after dismissing Pete Carroll. (photo by Jim Davis)

different things. 'On this play do this, if they do this we do that. If they do this, we do something else. If this happens, this happens. If that happens, something else happens.' Okay, but now we come to the game. All right, forget about all that. What do we need to do here to win? What are the most important things that we have to do here to win? We know there are 1,000 things we've talked about and everything is important but in the end let's get back to what we need to do here tomorrow."

FINAL PREPARATIONS

"Friday is certainly a coming together time and Saturday a lot of times is just a further coming together or further solidifying. Maybe we put some things on the back burner: 'We've got this if we need it. We've got that if we need it. If this situation comes up this is how we're going to handle it, but this is what we're going to go with. Here's how we're going to play the game.' Now if we have to adjust it, we adjust it. Because when you go through all of that in the beginning of the week the players really don't know—and sometimes the coaches don't know for sure, either—exactly how it's going to unfold.

"To just identify and get everybody on the same page—'Okay, here's how we're going to start so let's don't get confused with this other stuff. If we need it we'll come to it, but that's not what we're going to lead with.' So then the players can really zero in on, 'Okay, those calls, those adjustments… if this is called and that happens here's what we're going to do. There's another play where that might happen, but that play is 40 plays down the road. That's not what we're thinking about right now."

SATURDAY PREPARATION

"The game plan is pretty much done by Friday. Friday afternoon we're on the plane. We have a walkthrough practice on Saturday. There's not a whole lot of game planning going on. Maybe you prioritize some of the calls you want to make. 'Do we want to make this first? Do we want to call this first and then come with that? Do we want to call that first and then come back?' That type of thing. But I would say more so it's just getting caught up on a lot of little loose-end things that come up, getting ahead on the next team. Watching film, breaking down the next team you're going to play, or some of the coaches that are involved in the pre-scouting preparation. And for the play callers, more of prioritizing calls and making sure, thinking about the Saturday morning and night meetings. How you want to present the thing to the team, what reminders and what priorities, what film you want to show, and so forth.

"It's pretty standard. Whether we play home or away, the Saturday routine is the Saturday routine and that follows up off what happened Wednesday, Thursday, and Friday. What's the best way to bring everything together on Saturday prior to the game so you put your team in the best possible mindset and state of preparation for Sunday? 'Here's what we're going to call. Here's what we're going to do. We're going to save this. This is our adjustment if they do that. Here's how we're going to start the game. When they give us this look, here's what we'll do and that type of thing.' Make sure everybody's on the same page."

OUTDOORS ONLY

"When I first started coaching, there were no indoor options. At the Colts we were [usually] in Memorial Stadium, which wasn't a great practice facility because they sodded the infield after the baseball season and that area was all roped off. So you couldn't practice at that end of the field. You had to practice at the other end. Or the other option was you could push the WALK button and walk the team across the street to Eastern High School. On the field there—I would say it was two percent grass and 90 percent dirt and glass and rocks—and practice over there. So that's what it was. There was no indoor facility at Denver. There was no indoor facility at the Giants. We practiced every day, obviously, outside, like in training camp. So the world of the NFL now is a lot different than what it was."

WEATHER FORECASTS

"When you play in New England, you have to be ready for everything. I'd say based on the forecasts we've gotten so far this year [2014] none of them have been even close to what the game conditions were. There was 100 percent chance of rain last week and the only water I saw was on the Gatorade table. You know, it is what it is… I'm not saying I could do better than them [meteorologists]. It's just that they're wrong a lot. That's a fact. They're wrong a lot."

WEATHER PREDICTIONS

"I'm no better weatherman than you are or anybody else. As you get closer to the time you play then you usually have a more accurate assessment of it. I've made the mistake of telling a team too far in advance, 'Well, it looks like it's going to snow or rain or be hot or be cold' and then you come around to game time and it's the exact opposite. It's just a waste of time and the players look at you like, 'You're really on top of it this week, Coach.' I've kind of gotten out of that business. We've been out here at practice. We've practiced in rain. We've practiced in wind. We've practiced on hot days and we'll practice on cold days before the season is over."

WEATHER FACTOR

"In the end, whatever the conditions are out there, the team you're playing is the team on the other side of the line of scrimmage. That's who you have to beat. It's not like golf where you're hitting the ball into the elements. There's somebody on the other side of the line of scrimmage. You have to block and tackle, cover and defend and all that. [Weather] is certainly a part of the game… it's a factor, but I don't think it's as much of a factor as the execution of your team against your opponent. That's who the real opponent is."

ADJUSTING TO WEATHER CHANGES

"It certainly affects the kicking game first and then the deep passing game second and then everything else third…. I'm always hesitant to talk to the team about that too far in advance because then when you are wrong you've just wasted a lot of time talking about a situation that—guess what?—is not the way it is."

WEST COAST TEAMS PLAYING IN THE EAST

"These guys have all played in cold weather. They've all played on the East Coast. They've all played in those kinds of situations. It's not like it's high school and this is the first time we've gotten on a plane or something. This is the National Football League."

10-GAME ASSESSMENT

"There are a number of things that fundamentally change going into the second half of the season. The opponents, there's some different matchups. The weather could be a little bit more of a factor than it was earlier in the year. Situationally, we've all put our cards on the table. There's been enough situations in the first 10 games where you know everybody has had to show what they want to do in certain situations. Now all of that is out there and you're at another stage where, do you want to do the same thing in those situations or do you want to have a little bit of a change? Do you want to give them something else to think about or do you want to go back and rely on what you've practiced the most?

"You're in a different phase there on some things like that. Your fundamental offensive, defensive, and special teams core systems we've been practicing a long time and played a lot of games. I don't think you want to make too many changes to those but there's some subtle modifications that you make along the way, that the opponents make along the way based on what they're seeing from you, that you're into a little bit of that type game that I don't think you were into in the first few weeks of the season. You work on those situational things and they come up and you go with what you practiced. Now, for the most part everybody's seen that. We've seen what theirs are, they've seen what ours are. Now, where do you go from there?"

DECEMBER RECORD

Since Tom Brady became starting quarterback in 2001, the Patriots are 58–11 in games played in December, the final month before the postseason. The club has missed the playoffs only twice, in 2002 and in 2008, when Brady was out for the rest of the season after injuring his knee in the opener.

"I'd like to think there's a lot of pride taken around here in every game, including December.... We try to take pride in our performance every week, from Game 1 to Game whatever. That's the way we do it. Come in, prepare for the team, get ready to go, try to play our best on Sunday, and try to win. That's what we do every week. I don't have any real formula for why, but the most

Belichick and Tom Brady embrace after the most unlikely Super Bowl triumph over Atlanta in 2017. (photo by Stan Grossfeld)

important thing is that we maintain consistency there and we try to get to the highest level of consistency that we can. I'm not saying we always do it. We're far from perfect. We make a lot of mistakes but that's what we try to do. We try to do it on a regular week. It's not like we go along in October and November and say, 'Okay, we're going to really change things here in December and try to start playing good football.' We try to play good football all year long. We try to coach well. We don't always do it, but we're trying."

CHAPTER 6

Opponents

AS THE SON OF AN ASSISTANT COACH WHO LITERALLY wrote the book on football scouting, Bill Belichick is renowned for his meticulous preparation for the Patriots' opponents. "We don't have a 162-game schedule," he said. "We play 16 games. Every one of them is a big game. They're all urgent. They're all important. You don't get any of them back."

Belichick and his assistants make a point of knowing every starter, every backup, and every special teams player on the rival roster. "We have an individual scouting report on each player that plays on every one of those teams," the coach said. "What their tendencies are, what their strengths are, what we think their weaknesses are, and how to play them."

Belichick and his staff catalogue several thousand plays that opponents have used in recent seasons even though they know that they probably won't see more than 70. "We don't just want to say, 'Well, that's not going to come up,'" he said. "I think that would be irresponsible."

In a league that, from drafting to scheduling, has been designed to produce parity, preparation is paramount. "Every week you're up against a team that has the same opportunity as you do, the same salary cap, same draft choices," said Belichick. "Every week it's a huge challenge to be able to compete against that team. That's what it's about for me."

IDENTIFYING WELL-COACHED TEAMS

"The adjustments that they make. How well their players, as a group, play fundamentally. How well they handle situations—down and distance, time, things like that. It's not so much about the play. A lot of that is just having the right distribution, doing the right thing, and doing the right thing in a situation when the quarter-back scrambles, when stuff happens—screen passes, misdirection, deceptive plays, things like that. How the defense plays them. How well the offense executes them. How often they have obvious miscommunications where something is wrong. You don't know exactly what it is, but you know something is fouled up, versus the defense gives the offense a bunch of different looks, different situations, and they can handle it. Obviously they're doing a lot of things right."

DIVISIONAL INTENSITY

"We don't have a 162-game schedule. We play 16 games. Every one of them is a big game. They're all urgent. They're all important. You don't get any of them back. You only get 16 chances in the regular season. For us, every game is a big game. Obviously, division games are a little bit bigger because of the importance of the standings and what they mean to the division, but every game is a big game. Last week was a big game. Next week will be a big game. They're all huge. Division rivals, those games are intense. Both teams know each other well. They know their schemes. They know the players. They've really played against each other so there is a high level of competitiveness there. That high level of competitiveness is there in the other games as well. This one you just know each other a little better, that's all. You're more familiar with them.

"The Jets are tough. I'm sure they think we're tough. That's the way it is in this division. You play tough games in the division. It's highly competitive and the week leading up to it is an intense week. You want to try to get everything right. You know they've got all the tips on you. You think you've got all the tips on them. You want to try to balance those out and attack their weaknesses and exploit your strengths. That's the matchup every week there."

DIVISIONAL OPPONENTS

The Patriots have been playing their three AFC East opponents—the Bills, Dolphins, and Jets—home and away since the AFL and NFL merged in 1970, and have met Buffalo and New York ever since the inaugural AFL season in 1960. During Belichick's tenure (through 2017), New England has an aggregate regular season record of 80–28 against those rivals and has won 15 divisional titles, the last nine of them in a row.

"We have all of this year's information. Then we have our two games against them last year. Then we have all the games that we had from last year going into our games…. It's a couple thousand plays on offense, a couple thousand plays on defense. It's probably 700–800 plays in the kicking game. It's a lot of plays. They can't do everything that they have shown, but you have to be ready for it because they have it and they've done it and we know they have it.

"I think it's trying to whittle down the volume of information, which is excessive. It's way more than you need, but you can't ignore it. If they did something in the past, we can't ignore it. Or if they've had a strong tendency of doing something in the past but they haven't done as much of it recently, but they've shown it, we know they still have it. We don't just want to say, 'Well, that's not going to come up.' I think that would be irresponsible. But at the same time, you can't get ready for everything. There's just too much history.

"As a coach and player you've got to focus on a few key things and make sure you get those done. Every defense can't stop every play that they've shown. Every play can't block every defense that they've shown. It's impossible. But you have to put your chips on some number and go

Belichick salutes the fans after the home playoff victory over Baltimore during the 2014 season. (photo by Matthew Lee)

with that and then be ready to adjust during the game when you see things declare.

"Or maybe they've got three or four different ways to play a certain look. How have they chosen to play it this week? We've seen these two or three things but it looks like it's going to be more like this particular version and we have to adjust to that. It's a different dynamic than playing a team that you're trying to get familiar with, [a team] you don't know everything about…. Rarely do we come out of games saying, 'We've never seen them do that before.' That's usually not what we're saying."

FACING A DIVISIONAL
RIVAL THE SECOND TIME

Though the Patriots have owned a lopsided advantage over AFC East opponents under Belichick, their record in the second meeting of the season is exceptional—a combined 41–15, including 11–3 following a loss in the first meeting.

"There's some recall. I think you still need to go through the process because each team is different. There are situational plays and their down-and-distance tendencies and formations and, of course, they keep doing things to disguise it and change it up as we do, as every team does. But I think the big thing is you know the personnel. You know the players. You've played against them, you've matched up against them and you know what their strengths and weaknesses are, or you know how you match up against those individual players. I would say there are not a lot of players playing in this game that didn't play in the last one a month ago. The Xs and Os, the schemes, the formations—those matchups always change a little bit. But I think it does help you to know the players and how they use them and what their roles have been through the course of the year. Whether they used them that way in the last couple of weeks or so, you still know that's basically the guy's role on the team and you can prepare for it."

OPENING-GAME UNPREDICTABILITY

The Patriots are 13–5 in opening games in the Belichick era. After dropping three of their first four, they won the next 10 in a row.

"Each team has held things back in preseason, whether that's by design or whether it is just by the sheer number of plays that your top players have played together. So even if you play a quarter in the first game, a half in the second game, three quarters in the third game, and a quarter in the fourth game, you still won't even have two full games. So how many plays can you run? How many things can you show, even if you're not really trying to hide a lot? Everybody will keep a few things back. You keep things back, they keep things back, and then you go out there in the opener and you have a multiple of things that we haven't practiced against or that they haven't practiced against. So how will it all match up? At the second week, you at least get a look at the first week where nobody's holding back anything. There's less out there.

"There's always something new in every game, but the more that gets out there the easier it is to prepare for

The coach during one of his less voluble moments with the media before the Super Bowl duel with the Seahawks. (photo by John Tlumacki)

it. I'm not saying the easier it is to defend, but the easier it is to prepare for because at least you've seen it. But I think the multiples are what really get you. At Kansas City [under Andy Reid], you don't really know what personnel group they're going to be in. You don't know what formation they're going to be in. The plays that they've run basically will be the plays that they'll run, but we don't know how they'll build them or how they'll create them. I'm sure they'll have some new plays. That's hard to get ready for from their standpoint. I'm sure they'll look at us and say, 'Well, we've got 19 games last year, and some games we're in this, some games we're in that, and some games we're in something else.'

"So they're trying to get ready for a pretty broad base, kind of like what we are on offense. We watched all of Kansas City's games from last year. Some games they're doing more of this, some games they're doing more of something else, so what are you going to get? Do you spread yourselves thin and work on a little bit of everything? Or do you put more eggs in one basket and say, 'Well, we really think they're going to do this,' and concentrate on one particular area here? Then you better hope you're right. That's opening day and it's a lot harder to figure that out than it is after two or three regular season games that you've watched from experience."

PREPARING FOR NEW WRINKLES

"It's hard to have like 10 new runs every week. Usually what you have is maybe one new run, but sometimes the runs that you have that are your core plays, you try to disguise and run differently. Either different personnel, maybe a different formation, maybe change the look a little bit so that the defense doesn't see the play until right when or after the ball is snapped, as opposed to being able to look at it for five or six seconds and say, 'Okay, here comes the lead or here comes the power or here comes the counter,' or whatever.

"What we need to do defensively is understand the basic concept of the play, knowing that they can get to it in a lot of different ways. They can build it formationally, they can build it from different personnel groups, but in the end here are the basic blocking schemes, this is what we have to defeat. Can we guess which way they're going to run it? Probably not. But their basic core plays from different looks, can we recognize those after the snap? Hopefully, yes, that's the idea.

"When you go back to Washington's offense—Joe Gibbs was there when I was at the Giants—they really had only three plays, but the plays were the plays. But it's unbelievable the amount of success they had running the inside zone, running the outside zone, and running the counter OT. And all three plays kind of looked the same. They could pretty much do all of them out of the same or very similar looks. They complemented them well. Those were the ones you had to stop. There might be one or two other things sprinkled in, but that had to be 90 percent of it. They won a lot of games doing that."

FAMILIAR COORDINATOR, NEW TEAM

"Any time a coordinator changes, you go back to your notes for that coordinator, with the team he was at and what he did there. That travels with the guy. Sometimes that stays the same. Sometimes it gets modified a little bit. Sometimes it changes. Depending on who the head coach is, you just have to look at it. Sometimes it matches up pretty cleanly. Sometimes part of it matches up, like maybe it's the third-down package but their base defense is different or vice versa. You see certain elements of it. Maybe the pressures are the same but the zone coverages are a little bit different or whatever it happens to be.

"The same thing in the kicking game, offense, defense. I think you definitely want to track those guys. That's part of what you do in the off-season. You look at your opponents on the schedule. You look at coordinators who have changed or maybe a particular person that's been added to the staff. Maybe it's not even a coordinator but a new

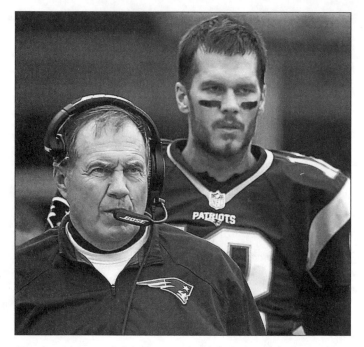

Coach and quarterback observe the defense at work during the 2015 home triumph over the Jets. (photo by Jim Davis)

offensive line coach… that guy might have his protection system or he might have his running game, certain schemes, or that type of thing. You see that scheme element has been added and then as you go through the year and you look at it you say, 'Okay, how much of an influence is this? Yeah, we know they have that, but they're not using it a lot. It looks like this guy is running his protections and maybe the coordinator is running his pass patterns, or whatever it is.'"

WHODUNIT

"A lot of times you don't know exactly who's doing what, but you just see what the team does and that's what you prepare for. So whether it's a quarterback, an offensive coordinator, a head coach, the offensive line coach in the running game or the same people on the defense and special teams—coordinator, head coach, specialists, signal caller, key guys. However it all comes out, the bottom line for you is that's how it comes out. So the inner workings of who actually does what, whose call it is and so forth, doesn't matter as much to us as what the final result is of what we have to defend or what we have to deal with. What we try to identify is how they play certain situations, what their strategy is or what they're going to present to us that we have to deal with. However that comes out, whoever called it or set it up and strategized it, that means a lot less to us than what they actually do."

PREPARING FOR SPECIFIC PLAYERS

"We prepare for all guys on the active roster. We just don't prepare for one guy. It wouldn't make any difference.... It's like that at every position. We know who the players are, we know who the backups are based on what we know, what we've seen, what we anticipate to happen. Who would be the next perimeter corner? Who would be the next inside corner? Who would be the next safety? Who would be the next dime guy? Maybe they wouldn't use dime, maybe they'd use nickel. Who would be the next nickel guy?

"Whatever it is, we have to be ready for that. It's one play away from happening. We always prepare for all the players who are on the active roster. Then we come to the game and before the game we cross off the seven guys who are inactive. So, okay, this week they only have two tight ends active or they only have five linebackers. Or, here are the guys who are inactive, whether they're injured or whether they're inactive for other reasons, whatever it happens to be…. Maybe that gives us an indication, a little bit more information of maybe what type of game it might be. If a team has extra DBs active for our game and maybe less defensive linemen, maybe that's an indication that it's going to be more of a nickel game.

"Or, vice versa, a team keeps extra tight ends and running backs and fewer receivers, maybe it's an indication that they're going to try to play bigger, that type of thing. But until that point, we work with everybody. I know a lot of people who live and die on the injury report but I don't really care what's on the injury report. Look, I don't know how these guys are going to be, either. We can put down whatever we want. But they're humans—some get better, some stay the same, some don't get better. There is no way to know for sure and there are a lot of times it comes down to game-time decisions. I'm saying that about our team and I'm with them and I'm talking to our doctors and trainers every day.

"But other teams, they're going through the same thing, too. Just because a guy is on the injury report and whatever he's listed as, that doesn't really mean anything. Guys that aren't well can make quick recoveries. Guys that are well can not turn the corner. So we're ready for those guys, too. Honestly, I don't even care what's on the injury report. I really don't even look at it. Unless a guy is definitely out, then okay. If he's not, then to me we've got to be ready for him."

TRACKING SPECIAL TEAMERS

"We try to know where every player is going to be on special teams. We go through every player on the kickoff team, what their strengths and weaknesses are, where they line up, if they move around, if they are usually in the same spot, who the safeties are, who the contain guys are, who the first guy down is, which guys play behind. Somebody is the first guy down. Somebody plays behind them. Some guys go to the ball. Some guys are more lane players. Absolutely, we go through that every week, every game, and we do the same thing on the punting game, punt returns, and kickoff. We have an individual scouting report on each player that plays on every one of those teams: what their tendencies are, what their strengths are, what we think their weaknesses are, and how to play them."

CHANGING GAME PLANS

"I think you can change certain elements from week to week, but it's hard to change everything every week. Some teams, if they are going to change certain things then other things stay the same. Like maybe their two-minute offense, their goal-line offense, their red-area offense, or their third-down offense. Then they change something else, like their first-down offense, or they change their third-down offense but they keep their running game the same, or they change their running game but they basically keep their red-area the same.

"It's hard to change your entire offense every week, but I think if you play a 3-4 team then these are the runs we're going to run against a 3-4 team. If you play a 4-3 over-and-under team, well, here are the runs we're going to run against a 4-3 over-and-under. They might be completely different. You see teams do that, but if they do that then they probably don't change everything else. You see some teams pretty much run the same runs every week but depending on what coverages you play.

"If you're a zone team then they have this set of patterns. If you are a man team then they have this set of patterns. If you are a pressure team then they have another set. If you're a quarters team then they have another set. Now if you mix it up then they mix it up. It's like they have a little block on their game plan. If you're playing Cover 2, we run this. If you're in Cover 3, we run that. If you blitz, we run this. Other teams do it by protection. It's hard to give a specific answer to that. I think what you have to do each week is figure out what their formula is, what they're going to change and what they're not. What their philosophy is in certain situations, on certain plays, or certain groupings. Sometimes it revolves around them and sometimes it revolves around the defense."

CHANGING GAME PLAN
AFTER INACTIVES LISTED

"I guess it would depend on what's on that list, but I'd say probably not too much. Look, you know a lot more after two series into the game than you will after looking at that inactive list. Obviously if there was a player that was a critical player for you in your game plan that wasn't going to play then maybe that would alter something a little bit. You're going to double a receiver and the receiver is inactive for the game then, 'Okay, we're not going to double him.' That knocks that call out. Do you replace that with a different call or do you go to the next guy? Or do you just say, 'Okay, we're not going to double anybody. Here's what we're going to do.'?

"But I'd say those situations are not that frequent. If you had that situation going into the game like, okay, this guy has a bad hamstring, not sure whether he'd be ready to go or not, then we're going to sit there and say, 'All right, if the guy plays, then here's what we're going to do. If he doesn't play or maybe he doesn't play all the time because we know he's dealing with something, maybe he's in on some plays and out on some plays, then we wouldn't game plan him when he's not on the field.

"There really aren't too many of those situations where, out of the blue, somebody that you think is going to play [who's] a very significant part of the game plan totally catches you by surprise. But if that were to happen—say a guy got suspended or he had a family member die or came down with some bug or something the day before the game—it's no different than if he got hurt on the second play of the game. You make that added adjustment."

RIVALS' OPENING SERIES

"Some teams have a game plan, whether it be on offense or defense, and they start out playing that game plan…. Halftime adjustments, I mean, that's ridiculous. Why wait 'til halftime? There it is. The first series of plays you can see what they're going to do, so you better start dealing with it. There are other teams that maybe anticipate that you're going to play a certain way and they script the plays, and a lot of times the scripts are to break their tendencies like, 'Okay, we've done this so we're going to start the game and show this, but do that. We want to get the ball to this guy because we want to try to get him going, so we're going to put this play in.'

Belichick barks instructions during 2017's victory at New Orleans. (photo by Jim Davis)

"So maybe those first few plays are just how they want to start the game. Maybe that's not really the game plan at all. Maybe that's just they want to break their tendencies. They want to show you something. They want to throw a deep pass to back the corner off so they can throw in front of him. They want to throw a quick pass to get the corner up so they can throw behind. So sometimes those plays are significant in terms of, 'Okay, here's the way it looks like they're going to play us.'

"Sometimes it's not. Sometimes a team will come out and play zone coverages the first few plays to see what kind of formations you're using, see how you're trying to attack them offensively, and then once the game gets going, then, 'Okay, here they are, let's go after them,' that type of thing. It doesn't always declare that way. A lot of times those first few plays are just a little bit of mirage. You've got to be careful about [thinking], 'This is the way it's going to be,' when really that's not the case at all. That's just the way they want to start the game. That's not really the way they want to play the game. I don't think there is any set book on that."

TRAVEL PLANS

While the Patriots know years in advance that they'll be boarding planes for New York (actually, New Jersey), Buffalo, and Miami every season, their non-divisional road schedule varies each year. Last season (2017) they played in New Orleans, Tampa Bay, Denver, Pittsburgh, and Mexico City (against the Raiders). This year (2018) they'll travel to Jacksonville, Tennessee, Pittsburgh, Chicago, and Detroit.

"As much as we can we try to stay in a routine. If you try to change your travel plans in a week you're trying to ship, whatever it is, 200 people out to wherever you are—players, coaches, staff, marketing, equipment, everything else. Whatever the FAA regulations and so forth are—I mean, you can't just throw whatever you want on an airplane now. You've got weight requirements, you've got packing requirements, things like that.

"There are things that we did years ago, even as little as a couple of years ago, that we can't do any more. A lot of times we truck our equipment to the away sites. There are issues with smaller planes and weight and cargo and baggage. Look, we're moving a lot of people here. Every once in a while something comes up. Like when we played Pittsburgh in the AFC Championship Game [in 2004] and we had the snowstorm. We left a day early and went up there. You see what your options are and make the best of them. Sometimes there's availability and sometimes there isn't and then you figure out what the next-best thing to do is. But we're not in an environment where whatever we want to do, 'Okay, let's do that.' There are a number of hoops to jump through."

ADJUSTING TO STADIUMS

"I think it's the same every week whether you've been there or not. Of course if you haven't been there [then] there is a newness to it but even if you have been there at most you're probably playing in that stadium once a year. So just re-familiarizing yourself with the conditions, the sun, the lights, the scoreboard, the 40-second clock—I would say in most of those stadiums the way they're built there's a difference in the wind between in the end zone where it's more protected and out at midfield and usually the flags are no indicator of anything other than it's the opposite of whatever they are. The turf, the footing, the consistency of that if cleats are an issue.

"If it's a turf field then obviously it's not the case, but if it's not, then what are the conditions? Cleveland's surface versus Arizona's surface—I mean, they couldn't be more different. Each game is different, so even if you've been in that stadium before, if it's a day game, if it's a night game, whatever the wind is, whatever the sun is, it's different for that day. I think fundamentally you always want to go through that process and re-acclimate yourself to the specific conditions for that particular game."

GRIDIRON QUIRKS

"Those old fields like Veterans Stadium [in Philadelphia] that were baseball fields where they would take out the pitcher's mound and put in a square of turf that they would inlay in there, [there were sometimes] some bad seam areas in various spots. Definitely, players were aware of that. They're not looking at it, they're playing, but there's some awareness of it. A lot of times the sidelines, when you have a multi-purpose field, there are multiple markings out there. We had that when I was in Denver in the old Mile High Stadium where the Denver Bears played. The first-base line ran not quite parallel to the sideline and so it was lighter, but you could still kind of see it, and the way it was cut it was clearly there, but the sideline was a little bit farther. I remember we had a couple of plays out there, one in particular, where a runner thought he was out of bounds and he got hit and it was a yard sale—helmet, ear pads, chin strap. Each stadium has its own little idiosyncrasies and uniqueness."

CROWD NOISE

"There are plenty of times on the road offensively that the crowd noise isn't an issue and there are plenty of times at home when crowd noise isn't an issue. But there

Belichick responds to queries before the 2016 AFC title game with the Steelers. (photo by Barry Chin)

are times when it is. You just have to be prepared on that side of the ball. Whichever side of it you're on, whichever game you're playing, you're going to have to deal with it at some point. But it's not 100 percent of the time on every play, in my experience. Except if you get into a game at a neutral site like the Super Bowl, then you kind of have noise on every play all the time. The decibel level goes up and down, but it's always pretty high. There is no home team. But that's obviously much more of an exception than the rule."

NOISY STADIUMS

"Seattle has always been one of the noisiest places, but you get stadiums like RFK [Washington] or old Mile High [Denver] where the seats were aluminum and they would beat on them and it was like 60,000 sets of cymbals going off at the same time. Literally, the whole stadium was reverberating, particularly in Denver."

OAKLAND'S BLACK HOLE

Once the Raiders returned to Oakland after 13 seasons in Los Angeles, a raucous cadre of fans took possession of seats in a Coliseum end zone and turned it into the Black Hole, whose denizens garb themselves like a cross between Star Wars figures, zombie clowns, and S&M devotees, all in silver and black. Still, the Patriots since have won two of their three meetings there with the Raiders.

"We don't get a very good reception out there, but that's the way it is just about every place we play. That's what playing on the road is. You have to be able to handle those elements, the hostile environment, the crowd noise offensively, just the fact that all you have are the people standing there on your sideline. That's the way it is just about every away game. We just have to block out all the support that our opponents are getting at home and focus on what our job is and make sure that our communication, our substitutions, and our execution during the game is the best that it can be. Just control what we can control. There's nothing we can do about the rest of that stuff. We know it will be what it is. You've all seen that before."

EVERY GIVEN SUNDAY

"It's a challenge. That's what this business is, it's challenging. There's definitely a thrill, there's an excitement if the results are good on Sunday—but sometimes they are, sometimes they aren't. We've seen the highs and lows of that. Every team will have that every season. The challenge is the competitiveness. You're up against the best players, the best coaches, the best organizations in football…. That's the way it is in the NFL. Every team is good. Every team has good players, good coaches, good scouts, good everything. If you're not at your best then you don't have any chance. If you are at your best, you might run into their best.

"This isn't like college where you can play down a couple of divisions on your schedule and that kind of thing. Every week you're up against a team that has the same opportunity as you do, the same salary cap, same draft choices. The way it's structured it's very, very competitive. Every week it's a huge challenge to be able to compete against that team. That's what it's about for me."

CHAPTER 7

Offense/Defense

DURING THEIR BEST SEASONS, THE PATRIOTS USUALLY have ranked at or near the top of the league in most points scored and fewest allowed. For Bill Belichick, the balance between a productive offense and a stingy defense is crucial to victory.

"Defensively you always like to be on a long field and just play the percentages," he said. "And conversely, putting the offense on a short field works in the offense's favor. Field position is always a critical thing."

For the offense, communication along the line and between the quarterback and receivers is vital to sustaining drives, as is taking advantage of individual matchups. For the defense, denying big plays and shutting down opponents inside the 20-yard line are essential. "Those are always two big points of emphasis every week," observed

Belichick. "Not to give it all up in one play and to play well in the red area and hold them to field goals."

FIELD POSITION

"Defensively you always like to be on a long field and just play the percentages. It forces the offense, if they don't get it all on one big play, to execute more plays throughout the course of the drive and statistically we all know that the further away they are from the goal line, the lower the percentages are that they'll score touchdowns, field goals, and points. That doesn't ensure anything.

"Defenses give up long drives and they give up big plays, but statistically speaking on a percentage basis, that field position works in the defense's favor. And conversely, putting the offense on a short field works in the offense's favor. Field position is always a critical thing. We had a situation come up at the end of the half where one first down, a few yards, makes a difference between a field goal or a scoring opportunity at the end of the half. You can score at the end of the half and then there's 1:30, 1:40, whatever left, and with good field position you or the other team can be right back in scoring position in a hurry. A few yards makes a difference then between a long field goal attempt and a Hail Mary into the end zone, which is a lower percentage play."

TURNOVERS FOR TOUCHDOWNS

Fumbles and interceptions lose games and damage playoff hopes. So Belichick puts enormous emphasis on ball security, and the Patriots during recent seasons have been first or second in the league in fewest turnovers.

"You have so many possessions in a game. You have eight to 12 or 13 possessions, depending on the length of those drives and the time they consume and so forth. So if we each had eight possessions and you score on a return when I have the ball then I've lost a possession and now I have to make it up the next time I have the ball or neutralize one of those scores. Statistically, it's hard to do. You look at all the times that happens, there aren't that many of them. So when you give one up it's a lot to overcome, because you only get the ball so many times.

"It's not like basketball, where you're going to have 70 possessions. You give up a turnover and you're going to get the ball another 69 times or whatever the average is in basketball. But in football you don't get it that many times, so to turn it over and to turn it over for a score.... What's the difference if you fumble the ball on the 10-yard line and they score on the next play or they intercept it and run it back for a touchdown? It's basically the same thing. It's kind of the same result, and that's why turnovers are so important. That's why they're so statistically heavily weighted toward the outcome of games. You don't have that many possessions. If you lose the ball and you give up points it's too hard to overcome. You might be able to get away with one of them, maybe, but it's hard to get away with more than that."

PLAY ACTION

"One of the best things about play action is the opportunity to really get receivers into some open space. When you just drop back and throw, whether you're throwing against man or zone, for the most part the defense is

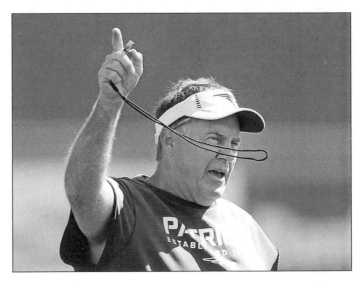

Belichick making a point during the 2016 training camp. (photo by John Tlumacki)

usually going to be fairly close to those guys, either matching them in zone or running with them in man-to-man.
Sometimes when you have a good play action and you're
able to displace the defense and get the linebackers coming
up or the secondary going back or get the linebackers or
whoever running inside while your receivers are running
outside you can create some space in the passing game,
that's much harder to get on a drop-back pass. That's the
advantage of doing it, and the running game helps the
play-action passing game. And then the play-action passing game helps the running game in terms of keeping the
linebackers from running up there quite so fast."

THIRD DOWN/RED ZONE SIMILARITIES

"The similarities are tight coverage. On third-and-3
to -6, -7, or -8, something like that, offensively you're
not expecting a lot of easy throws. It's not like first down,
where you might be able to complete a six- or seven-yard
pass that's not that heavily contested. Third-and-6, you
have to work for those. You either have to run a real good
route or you have to design a play that gets a guy open
in the defense. The defense isn't trying to give that up.
Coverage is tight on third down in those situations for
the most part and it's tight in the red area because you
don't have much field to work with.

"For a quarterback and a receiver, you've got to get open. The quarterback has to make a quick decision. He has to get the ball into tight coverage, and a lot of times it's a lot harder than on first and second down, where the defense is thinking about the run, maybe they have more run defenders on the field. You start putting five or six defensive backs out there and a good coverage linebacker, then they do some different things with their pass rushers and have a lot of different combinations of coverages they can go with, with all those defensive backs and linebackers on the field. It's hard to throw against even though you have your better receiving players out there. You have to see it quickly. You have to react and the ball has to be accurately thrown a lot of times for those plays to be successful. I'd say it's similar."

SWITCHING FROM OFFENSE TO DEFENSE

"At whatever point a coach takes a player from offense and puts him on defense, there is usually a reason for that. I would say the reason usually is that he's not enough of a playmaker on the offensive side of the ball. What coach is going to take your best playmaker and put him on defense? You just wouldn't do that, all things being equal. If the guy can't catch but he's a good athlete or he's everything but he doesn't have great hands, at some point you get a receiver who is a better pass catcher and you put this guy over on defense. You get a guy who is big and strong and tough but he's just not an elusive enough runner. He just can't run over everybody. You can run over guys who are smaller than you but at some point when everybody is the same size, you just can't run over those guys and he doesn't have the elusiveness.

"Then you put him over on defense and you get a more elusive running back, whether that's at high school, college, or wherever it is. I tell the defensive players all the time, 'Don't kid yourself. If you were a big enough playmaker you would have stayed on offense. They would have put you out there and you'd be having 100-yard receiving games or 150-yard rushing games.' It's like the defensive specialist in basketball. If you were that good of a shooter you'd be the point guard, but you're not. So start covering these guys or we'll get somebody else in there."

SWITCHING FROM DEFENSE TO OFFENSE

"Why does a coach move a player from defense to offense? It's usually speed. That's generally what it is.... You have a good football player. He's tough, he's physical, he's smart, he uses his hands well, he has good power, he has good balance, but he doesn't run well. What do you do with him? You make him an offensive lineman. That's his

Belichick in more formal attire before the Super Bowl against the Seahawks. (photo by Jim Davis)

last stop. I tell the offensive linemen that, too. 'If you could run you'd be on defense. Why are you on offense? Because you don't run well enough to play on defense.' Most of the time that's the truth—the defensive players run better than the offensive players."

LINE VERSATILITY

"There are a lot of guys who are tackles, there are a lot of guys who are guards, there are a lot of guys who are centers and that's the only position they play. Then you have some players who can play center and guard and then you have some players who can play guard and tackle. I don't want to say that they can't play center but that would be the least of the three. Trying to find the versatility of that player changes the makeup of your roster, particularly when you take seven linemen to a game. If you have a guard-tackle swing player then you could potentially go to the game with five inside players—your three starters, another inside player and then a guard-tackle swing guy as opposed to having just a three-position swing guy inside and then trying to find a swing tackle. Somewhere along the offensive line you have to have some position flexibility because nobody takes 10 offensive linemen to the game. You'd have a backup center, backup left tackle, backup right guard—you just can't do it. You have to find some versatility in there somewhere."

LINE CHEMISTRY

"We can all go out there and play together, but to actually play well and be able to pass things off like you have to do on the offensive line, [to] be able to communicate and see things the same way, that takes a lot of work, a lot of interaction, a lot of communication, a lot of trust. You have to trust that the other guy is going to be there to do what he's supposed to do so you do what you're supposed to do. You really have to trust each other on the line and know that the other person is supposed to be where he's supposed to be, so you can drop guys or pass guys or move on to your guys and know that you're protected in an area that you really can't look back and see and identify. You just have to trust that it's going to get done right. It's a hard thing to do."

BLOCKING

"Technique is important, willingness is important, but there are a lot of things that go on in blocking. Number one is doing the right thing, knowing who you have to block. A lot of times, blocking secondary players you have to make decisions as to which player to block. We always want to block the most dangerous guy, the guy that can get there first. Most of the time. Not all the time but most of the time.

"So that decision of, 'As I'm going to get this guy, is the guy that's on me going to get there before I get to that guy? Or do I turn back on him? Do I go get that guy who's lined up closer?' Those kinds of decisions—taking the right angle, blocking from in front not from behind because there are a lot of moving targets that they're blocking—those guys aren't always just standing there. Playing with good pad level and good leverage, not going in there and getting blown up by sometimes bigger guys they're blocking. A lot of it is desire, a lot of it is leverage, a lot of it is technique. Playing with a good base and getting your pad level down on contact and having your head in the proper location, things like that.

"I think that's an underappreciated part of [the tight ends' and receivers'] jobs. It's all about the stat sheet and fantasy catches or however that stuff works. But those guys go out there and compete every play and that helps a lot of other guys. That means a lot to our football team."

BACKUP QUARTERBACKS

With Tom Brady starting (and almost always finishing) games since 2001, his understudies rarely get off the sideline. Before he was traded to the 49ers in 2017, Jimmy Garoppolo had appeared in only 17 games in three-plus seasons and started only two. During the past decade, the Patriots usually have kept only one reserve quarterback, but he's aware that he could be under center at any moment. That's how Brady got the job, when Drew Bledsoe went down with a serious chest injury.

"When you're the backup quarterback you can go in after the first play like Matt Cassel did in 2008. You can go in on one of the last plays of the game like Tom Brady did in 2001 or somewhere in between. You never know as a backup quarterback. You have to be ready to go from the first play to the last one in all situations."

BACKUP QUARTERBACKS' PRACTICE ROLE

"They have a huge role in getting the defense ready to play, particularly trying to simulate not just the quarterback but the whole tempo and mannerisms of the offense. Cadence, shifting, motioning as well as the actual quarterback mannerisms and the way they read plays or execute them, trying to do it similar to the way that we are going to see it on Sunday…. That's when a quarterback can sharpen up some of his skills as well. You are working against the first defense and hopefully [defensive schemes] that are somewhat designed to stop what they're doing, so that the throws and the reads are tougher. Working against our defensive players doing our thing sometimes is a lot harder for a quarterback than running our offense against a defense that doesn't quite execute the other team's defense as well as what we're going to see on Sunday."

RUNNING BACKS

"The running backs have a tough job. They have to run the ball, find the holes, read the defense, and sort all that out. And in the passing game they have blitz pickup responsibilities and have to run routes against different defenses. Man, zone, when to break it, when to throttle down, when to accelerate, when to pull up, when to keep going, having to clear the line of scrimmage to get into the route and all those things. They are involved in every single play. It's like being the middle linebacker—there're no plays off. They have to do a good job on all those and a mistake can be costly. Missing a blitz pickup, ball handling, not running the right route, not catching the ball—any of those things can potentially be a big play. Those are critical jobs. I can't say, 'It's okay if we do okay on this but we can screw that up.' Everything's important."

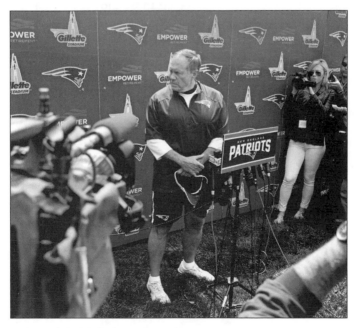

The coach holds forth outdoors during 2017's June minicamp. (photo by Jonathan Wiggs)

RUNNING BACKS' VISION

"A key to it is knowing when you have time to set blocks up and use the blocking scheme ahead of you to pull defenders one way or the other and cut off them, and when you don't and you just have to hit it and get through there because there's just not enough time. That's an instinctive thing that backs I'm sure learn through experience, and some have better than others.

"When you have that ability to have a little space and you have the patience to set up those blocks and force a defender to declare one way to set the block for lineman, guard, center, tackle, whoever it is—and then be able to cut off, that's really ideal. Sometimes you just don't have that luxury as a back. You have guys closing in on you and you just have to get through there and run with good pad level and get what you can.

"But patience is a key to that when used at the right time. We all hate to see the backs that run in there and have patience and then don't gain any yards. You want them to get the ball into the line of scrimmage and then go. So there's a fine line between when you have time to do that and when you don't."

JUDGING RUN QUALITY

"Just because it's not a 40-yard run doesn't mean it's not a great run. A lot of times the first guy who gets to him is 35 yards downfield. That doesn't make it a great run. There are a lot of five-yard runs where there's nothing there and the back gets five yards. Some of the best runs you'll see are five- [to] seven-yard runs. How does a guy get seven yards when you look at the play and there's nobody blocked? You think he's going to lose a yard or at best get back to the line of scrimmage, and he almost gets a first down.... Just because it's not a 50-yard run doesn't mean it's not a good run. You see plenty of them on film—breaking tackles, making guys miss, finding yards when it doesn't really look like there are many yards there. That's what good backs do. It's not just about how many yards a guy gains. You've got to look at the play."

FULLBACKS

"Most of the pure fullbacks in the NFL today, they're probably more like the quarterback in the single wing. They're almost like guards. They don't carry the ball very much. They catch a few patterns in the flat but they're really more blockers. Jim Brown—I'm not saying the guy couldn't block but the guy ran pretty well. When I first came into the league, most teams had a fullback who ran the ball and a halfback who ran the ball, the Sam Cunninghams of the world.

"Now, you very seldom see a fullback who has anywhere near the same number of carries that the running back has. What most teams have done, they've split those responsibilities and said, 'Okay, who is our best running back? That's the guy we want to have the ball. Let's give him the ball and let's get somebody else to block for him.' That has gone further to say, 'Well, we have a guy who can block for him and run the ball. We have another guy who can really block for him. Let's put the guy who's really a

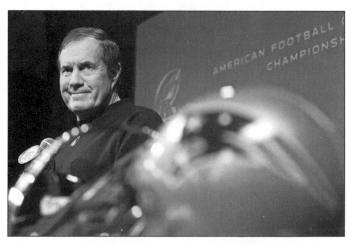

Belichick in a lighthearted mood before the 2011 AFC Championship Game with Baltimore. (photo by Bill Greene)

good blocker and we'll give our runner the ball a little bit more and give the other guy who carries it, give it to him a little less, and let's get someone in there who can really block.' A Lorenzo Neal–LaDainian Tomlinson situation. Neal is not going to have many carries, doesn't expect many, probably doesn't want many. Tomlinson is going to get by far and away the majority of them.

"You don't see the fullback-halfback combinations like you saw in the '70s, and you had to defend the fullback runs because fullbacks were good runners, as were the halfbacks. That's changed quite a bit. That's more of the Wing-T type of offense where you have inside runners, outside runners, that type of thing…. Once you got into the I formation, then you have a runner and a blocker. From there you took the fullback out of the formation and went to a one-back set, so you have a runner with either six guys in front of him or the seventh guy being a tight end who is a move tight end, the H-back and all that. That's been the transition."

TIGHT ENDS

"Generally speaking, the tight end could be the hardest position to match up on for a defense because it's hard to put a linebacker on the real good receiving tight ends like some of the guys we've seen—Tony Gonzalez, Jeremy

Shockey, Dallas Clark. It's hard for the linebackers to cover guys like that. And the defensive backs who have the speed to cover them, they're outweighed by 20, 30, 40 pounds and maybe give up two, three, four inches in height and length. So that's an issue. It's really hard to find a guy that's the same size as a Gonzalez or a Clark or Shockey that can cover them. You're either finding a smaller guy that can run with them or a bigger guy that can be physical with them but probably can't run or doesn't have their kind of quickness.

"So it's a tough matchup whereas the receivers and corners are much more matched physically. Every once in a while you see those big 6'4", 225-pound receivers that are hard to match up against. But for the most part those physical matchups are more in line than with a good receiving tight end. That's the challenge of those guys. They're really receivers in a tight end's body. Those are tough matchups."

PASS PATTERNS AND COVERAGES

"An awful lot of plays have guys running deep—post patterns, flag patterns, go routes, whatever it is. You don't throw them on every play but they're there on every play depending on what the coverage is and what the matchup is. If the quarterback sees it and the receiver runs a good route, then that's a good option. If the coverage takes that part of it away or they roll into that, then the quarterback reads the rest of his progressions.

"Sometimes you can play the percentages and think, 'Okay, there's a pretty good chance that we're going to get this pattern on this coverage.' Or if you run that pattern on this coverage, sooner or later you're going to get the coverage you're looking for and you're going to take a shot at it. But there's also plenty of times that we go out in practice and run plays and then we get in the game and we see something and it takes us to that and maybe we've practiced it and maybe we haven't. Say you run 100 plays during the week in practice—35, 35, and 30—and then you have goal-line plays and situational plays in there. And then you think of all the different coverages a defense can play on third down, on second down, on first down, in the red area.

"I understand they're only out there 60 plays, too, but you've seen on film, you've seen them play six, seven different sub coverages, a couple different blitzes, six, seven regular coverages… four, five blitzes on that. You go into the game with whatever number plays you have—the variables are just exponential. It's just so difficult to match up something unless you have a real strong tendency that they're going to do this when you give them a certain look or certain situation.

"I'd say that's maybe 10 percent of the time. It's not a high probability. You go out there and run your plays. You can't run them against all 10 different coverages that you could get in that situation. You run them against the ones you think are most likely or maybe what their tendency is or maybe what you think they'll do to you. But a lot of times it doesn't turn out that way and you have to adjust to it."

MATCHING RECEIVERS AND CORNERBACKS

"The advantages of it are that you get the matchup you want. You want this player covering that player, you got it. The disadvantage is, where do the other 10 players go? Normally that's not an issue because we just line up where we line up. But, 'Okay, now you're going to match up to so-and-so. So where do I go? All right, I take somebody else but what if he's not in the game? What if we're playing zone? What if this happens? What if that happens? What if this combination of guys is in the game? What if that combination of guys is in the game? Then who do we match up to? What if the guy that we're matching up to is out of the game, then who do you match up to and who do I match up to?' There's a lot of moving parts there.

"It's real easy to say we'll just take him but it's not that easy. I mean, if you just want to play One Coverage, but nobody does that. You've got zones, you've got mans, you've got combination man/zones, you've got blitzes, you've got zone-blitzes. So it's easy to match up and it's easy for that player. The hard part is, what does everybody else do, and we all have to wait and see where you go before we can all figure out where we go."

DEFENSIVE SCORES

"When you get points from a defensive score, you can't count on those points. You can't go into a game and think, 'All right, we're going to get seven points on a defensive score.' Over the course of the year, that maybe happens two or three times, whatever it is. So when you get those

A record five Super Bowl rings have earned Belichick the enduring faith of the Foxborough fans. (photo by Jim Davis)

in a game then that's pretty significant. The overall statistical advantage to scoring a non-offensive touchdown, that team is going to win more games.

"You put turnovers in there, you recover a fumble on the one-yard line—that's not a defensive score but if that ends up being a score you have a similar result. That's why the turnovers are so important, because they aren't always point plays but they usually result in points, especially if you get them in good field position. Then you're already in the scoring zone. A safety is part of that because even though it's only two points, it is possession, so it's a little bit of an added benefit."

DEFENSIVE MASKING

"It's got to be coordinated as a team. You can't have one guy disguising on things and somebody else disguising somebody else. A good quarterback would probably be able to figure out what you're trying to do and see that one guy is way out of position. You have to be very well coordinated on that because what they do with the cadence, they make it hard for you to do that. Sometimes they run up and snap the ball real quickly so it forces you to get lined up. Other times they go up there and they delay and check the play and get into a formation that makes you declare so they can see what you're in and then get to the play they want to get to and go at a very slow pace. It's hard to over-disguise because if they go quick then you could be way out of position."

DEFENDING THE NO-HUDDLE OFFENSE

"The biggest challenge is communication. They are used to running plays quickly, getting to the line, calling them and signaling them and not coming back to the huddle. Doing it from extended formations, getting lined up and going. Defensively we're used to doing it in an end-of-the-half type of situation, but on an every-down basis it stresses your communication and recognition a little bit. Making sure that you see the offense, see where they arc located because they will move them around. They don't just stay in the same formation all the time.

"Usually at the end of the half you see a lot more of that. You see more of the same formations because fighting time they don't want to take time to switch people around. Recognition and communication are two of the big things. And then you can't let the pace of the game and the communications challenges take away from actually playing, the technique, reads and doing your job. You can't let all that other stuff distract you. You get so caught up in that and the ball's snapped and you don't do anything."

A grim coach jogs off the field at halftime of the 2013 AFC title match at Denver, with his team trailing and headed for defeat. (photo by Jim Davis)

DEFENDING THE RED AREA

The red area [inside the 20-yard line, aka, the red zone] is where games primarily are won and lost. Holding an opponent to a field goal from there several times a game is a major factor in victories. The Patriots defense has improved markedly in that regard and last year ranked second in the league in points allowed per red-area trip [3.94].

"There's nothing more important than the red area. If you don't give up big plays they have to go through the red area to score, so if you don't give up big plays and you can play good red-area defense then it's hard for them to score a lot of points. Those are always two big points of emphasis every week—not to give it all up in one play and to play well in the red area and hold them to field goals.... Offensively, everybody's closer to the line, so the safeties are linebackers. Linebackers are, in a lot of cases, borderline defensive linemen. Everything's just compressed.

"So there are a lot of things you have to handle differently. Routes are different, coverages are different.... Generally you see more size in that area because there's less space, so speed is less of a factor. There's only so far you can run. Technique is important. Coordination is important. The proper spacing, the proper leverage, using the space that you have. Of course everything happens so much quicker down there because there's less space and less time so throws and catches have to be good. A lot of tight coverage, a lot of catches away from the body into a short space. Defensively, you're fighting for every inch, every yard. It's critical. Two yards at midfield is one thing. Two yards on the 5-yard line is 50 percent of the length, 50 percent of the field. So it's all heightened, it's all more urgent."

SECOND- AND THIRD-DOWN DEFENSE

"On first and second down the offense has a lot of options. They have one or two more downs so you can pretty much do any play you want. I don't think there's really anything that you can't do on first down. If you want to take a shot and throw one down the field and you hit it, great. If you don't, you still have two more downs to pick it up. Until you get into four-down territory, when third down could be like second down, third down is really a possession down. Then you have to get the yardage that you need offensively, and defensively you're trying to defend the yardage that they need to get. It's really a one-play series, not a three-play series."

NICKEL DEFENSE

"That's an every-week game-plan discussion. Do you want to match? Do you want to not match? Or, what situations do you want to match in? Or, are there some three-receiver sets you want to match, others you don't? Maybe who the tight end is, who the back is, maybe who the receivers are. Sometimes it's not always the same three guys. Maybe a certain receiver changes how you want to match up. Maybe it's by down-and-distance...

It's every week. It's how and when to match up with multiple-receiver groups and multiple–tight end groups as well."

FORCING A SECOND READ

"Anytime you can force a quarterback to make after-snap decisions and make multiple ones then you're on the right track. I don't understand playing defense and going back and letting the guys do what they want to do and have a field day. I don't think that's good defense. I can't imagine you'd want to do that against any team—young, old, anywhere in between."

INTERIOR LINE PLAY

"A lot of the interior game for the linemen is being able to recognize how much weight the guy has going forward, which might indicate whether he's going to penetrate or stunt. Or being able to recognize the width of the offensive line's splits or how far back they're sitting, if they're going to pull, a lot of little things like that.

"When you draw up the formation and put it on a scouting report, the formation looks the same, but the little variation of the lineman's weight distribution, his stance, his split, his depth, whether he's in a two-point stance or a three-point stance, sometimes how far back one of his feet is or the relationship of the guard and tackle on the side of the ball, that kind of thing. There are a lot of little things a lineman can pick up out there. They can pick it up during the game as they start to play against the player. You can't see that kind of detail on film. You're just too far away and the pictures are being taken from the top of the stadium and you just don't get it like you do when you're lined up a foot or two away from the guy.

"In terms of smarts—street smarts, instincts, recognition, whatever you want to call it—it's a lot of that. All the good defensive linemen I've ever coached would do things that at times would not really be their assignment on the play but it was because they knew what was happening based on the way a guy was leaning, or his stance or the split or something like that gave him a good indication of what to do. And that sort of trumps everything."

DEFENSIVE HOLDING

"There's not too much holding on defense. We're not trying to hold anybody. Do some of our guys get held? I don't know. I've heard people say you could call holding on every play and to a degree that's probably true. You probably could. But whatever the case is for a defensive player it still comes down to leverage, hand placement,

Belichick during a pensive moment during the 2009 exhibition season. (photo by Bill Greene)

and being able to control the guy who is trying to block you, and there is always somebody assigned to block you. That's the big thing for any defensive player but particularly a defensive lineman. What plays does an offense run where they don't block a defensive lineman? That guy is going to get blocked. It's just a question of whether he can defeat that block and control his area and then ultimately get off the block and make that play.

"So that's what a defensive lineman has to do. There are defensive players that talk about, 'Yeah, I like to be freed up. I'm good when I'm free.' Well, great, who isn't? The bigger part of it is being able to defeat somebody who is blocking you."

DEFENDING TWO RUNNING BACKS

"You just have to be disciplined in your reads. There's only one runner back there. If he's back there with a tight end or a fullback or something like that you know who the runner's going to be. It could be a pass but you know who basically is going to carry the ball. With two guys back there then misdirection plays and reading your keys and making sure that you defend your responsibility—because there's more than one guy that can carry it—becomes more critical, which is the way it was when I came into the league when there were two running backs. So the halfback blocked, the fullback ran [or] the fullback blocked, the halfback ran. Your keying system was, for linebackers, much more difficult then because of the different combinations of plays that they had.

"As that's evolved to a one-back set, for the most part we know who's going to carry the ball and so that's just changed a little bit. When you put two guys back there, especially if you're not used to doing it, understanding that there's probably not a lot of one guy-is-blocking-for-the-other guy plays, there's more of one guy runs here, the other guy runs somewhere else, which guy has the ball? You have to defend both of them as opposed to having lead blockers. I wouldn't say that that's featured, but when you have two guys going in different directions then that can slow down the defense."

TACKLING RUNNING BACKS

"Guys have different styles. Guys have different ways of breaking tackles. Defensively, that's an issue of knowing who you're tackling and how you want to tackle them...You're still going to make the tackle and there's fundamentals involved to tackling but different players have different strengths. Some guys are stiff-arm players, some guys drop their shoulders, some guys are jump-cut guys, some guys are spinners, some guys challenge your leverage and cut back.

"Other guys try to outrun you. So you've got to adjust and adapt. Look, the guy can do whatever he wants to do, so you have to tackle what it is. But you know their certain tendencies… ways guys like to run or carry the ball or break tackles. If you know that a guy's a spinner, then you tackle him a little bit different and with a little more awareness than if he's a guy that you know is going to always drop his shoulder and try and get low and try to grind out a few extra yards on contact. It's just a different running style. The guys that can do them all, they're obviously the hardest ones to tackle. They have multiple pitches they can throw and it's hard to hit them."

COVERING RUNNING BACKS
OUT OF THE BACKFIELD

"It could change a lot, depending on who the players are and how the offense uses it. Some offenses involve their running backs a lot in the passing game. Some of them use them more in protection and to run the ball and play action, things like that. Some guys, they're go-to guys in the passing game on third down and getting them the ball in space. Protection is another thing that varies from back to back. Some backs can do a lot of different protections.

The Super Bowl trophy in triplicate at the City Hall celebration after the improbable victory over Atlanta. (photo by Barry Chin)

"Some backs, it looks like teams just use one or two protections with them so that they don't have a lot of different assignments. Each week when the linebackers see who the backs are, or the secondary if they're involved in it, you definitely take more time to go through the scouting report with the backs. How they're used in the passing game, what kind of skills they have, some examples of them using those skills. Whether they're deep receivers, whether they run a lot of option-type routes, whether they're guys that can get open, whether they're more catch-and-run-type players, check-down receivers, things like that. Usually the player's skills will be complemented within the offense.

"If the back is a good route runner they'll probably run him on some man-to-man-type routes. If the back is more a catch-and-run guy they'll run receivers deep and let him be the check-down-type guy if it's zone coverage instead of asking him to win a lot of one-on-one situations if that's not really one of his strengths. It's definitely a key coaching point, particularly for the linebackers, and it could be in sub situations if you have a DB that's playing down close to the line of scrimmage. But covering those guys, what they do, how they do it, and what their skills are, there's a wide, wide range from real good to almost non-existent, guys that some teams hardly ever throw the ball to. So knowing who is in the game and what they're capable of doing and how we want to defend them is a key point every week. Very important."

SAFETY SKILLS

"There are certain skills at safety that are a little different than they are at corner. You see more of the field. You get a better chance to read the quarterback on a lot of things, depending on how much man or zone coverage you're playing. Your matchups are different on inside receivers versus perimeter receivers. Certainly the recognition and diagnosis of the play—the quarterback, the relationship between the receivers from the inside part of the field—is a lot different than it is from the outside part of the field. There's certainly a different perspective of the game from in there, there's no question about that."

FREE SAFETIES

"Those players don't get involved in every play but the plays that they are involved in are significant plays. They're open-field tackles. They're passes that are thrown a lot of yards down the field. They can be game-changing plays or game-winning plays. Turnovers, things like that. That's the nature of that position. It's not like playing guard or defensive tackle, where you're right in the middle of every play…. It's important when the opportunity comes that the player is able to make the play and do what he needs to do in that situation. It's different than some of the other positions on the field but critical once it comes up. Then it's the most important position on the field."

COMPETING FOR THE BALL

"Something that we work on from the first day of training camp is going up defensively and competing for the ball. Being in good position, that's part of the battle in the secondary, but that's the way it always is. Being in position is part of the battle and then finishing the play and making the play on the ball, that's the other half of it. The defensive back and the receiver, those guys have the longest play. The defensive linemen and offensive linemen aren't far apart from each other.

"A lot of times those plays are determined pretty quickly and then it's go to the ball. But in the secondary you have to play for three, four, five seconds. And then, in a lot of cases, it comes down to that last split second of whether it's a good play or a bad play. You could be in a perfect position defensively and mistime or miss the ball. Or offensively, you could not run a good route and not really be open but make a good catch. Or you can run a great route and do everything right and drop the ball. For those positions every part of the play is important, but the finish of the play is a lot of times what decides whether it's a good play or a great play or a bad play, and that's the position.

"It is hard to simulate but it's something that we always work on, finishing the play and being in position but also making the right judgment at that time. A lot of times you go up and you can't get the ball but the receiver has to bring it down and possess it. So it's not a catch until he comes down and brings it in. So even though you might get outrebounded, with good technique you still have a chance to get the ball out before he's able to control it."

CHAPTER 8

Special Teams

BILL BELICHICK'S FIRST OFFICIAL JOB IN PROFESSIONAL football was as a special teams assistant for the Lions. That was also his niche when he later signed on with the Broncos and Giants. As Patriots head coach, he continues to give exceptional value to all aspects of the kicking game and the impact that touchdowns produced by those units have on outcomes.

"In the National Football League, when you have roughly half of the games being decided by a touchdown or less, if you can get those seven points that you basically can't count on, that tilts a lot of games right there," he said.

Since numerous players perform on all four special teams, Belichick assigns them the same distinction that he does to offensive and defensive starters. Some, like Matthew Slater and Larry Izzo, were perennial Pro Bowlers.

"Those guys can make a great contribution to the team and be very valuable for it and have long careers," the coach observed. "Long snappers, guys like that. Some players really embrace that and can build on it and can have longevity doing it."

SPECIAL TEAMS SCORES

"Any time you get what I would call 'bonus points,' whether it's a defensive score or special teams score, the correlation between that and winning is high. I'm not sure if it's 90 percent, but it's definitely high. In the National Football League, when you have roughly half of the games being decided by a touchdown or less, if you can get those seven points that you basically can't count on, that tilts a lot of games right there."

EVOLUTION OF COACHING SPECIAL TEAMS

"I would say it's evolved a lot. You're playing some of your starters on special teams. You have six linebackers on the roster, four running backs, four receivers—well that's what they had, too [in 1977]. Now you have a lot more specialization. You have a lot of teams that have a core group of players in the kicking game, five or six guys that are pretty much on every team. Then you have your specialists and you have maybe a couple other guys that may play on one or two teams depending on what the needs of that team are. Obviously you can plan more smaller guys on punt return and kickoff coverage than on the punt team because you only have two guys split out there, right?

"So depending on which team you're talking about there's one or maybe two-phase players and then those four-phase players are usually four, five, six, seven players on your roster depending on how it's comprised in addition to the specialists. Definitely the players on the smaller roster, they were true backup players. They were one play away from playing middle linebacker or tight end or running back or corner or whatever. Now you see teams going into games with five safeties, five corners, five running backs. Heavier positions because there's depth there in the kicking game for those guys. Then schematically I'd say it's changed a lot just in terms of punt formation.

"The kickoffs have changed because of the ability of the kickers and the rules, where now it's a touchback game. The same thing on the field goals. It's hard to block field goals now because of the rules. Fifteen, 20 years ago, you had a lot of options. You could overload, you could load up certain spots in the protection. Now it's hard to do that. You can't hit the snapper, can't jump, can't push, can't pull. Yeah, it's changed."

SPECIAL TEAMS MENTALITY

"The best thing for a player is to really understand his role and maximize that. I think that all players want to go out there and do the best in all situations but not everybody is called on to do everything. Some guys have specific roles to do and once players identify how productive they can be in those roles and really work at them then they can build those roles into more than roles. They become core parts of your team. Some players understand that. Some players do that and they build on it.

The coach in mid-November garb during practice for the 2015 road date with the Giants. (photo by Barry Chin)

"I've seen other players who were good special team players maybe their first year or two in the league and they don't want to do that anymore. They want to go and try to have a bigger role on offense or defense, and then sometimes in two or three years they're out of the league. If they took a different approach, like guys who just build on establishing a bigger role for themselves on the team… whether it's a third-down back, a short-yardage back, a swing lineman, a third-down cover linebacker, whatever those roles are that aren't necessarily full-time unit roles, offensive or defensive roles. But those guys can make a great contribution to the team and be very valuable for it and have long careers. Long snappers, guys like that.

"Some players really embrace that and can build on it and can have longevity doing it and get better at it. Then there are some players that don't understand that is what their role is. They want their role to be something else, and then if they can't get to whatever that other one is sometimes end up with nothing. And that's unfortunate that sometimes that happens."

SPECIAL TEAMS INJURIES

"When you lose a player on special teams you really lose a starter on four teams at least. Sometimes you have one person that can replace the player, so it's Player A in for Player B. But a lot of times you have a combination of players where you either have to move somebody around or you use more than one player to replace that guy. It just depends on the player, but that's the challenge as a special teams coach, especially when it happens during the game. You lose somebody and then, okay, it's the kickoff team, the kickoff return team, the punt team, the punt return team. It's hard during the game, usually, to have one player that does all four of those.

"Maybe the next week if that player is out, if you have one person that can do that you might be able to make that guy active. But normally during the game you end up having to juggle some balls there, 'Okay, you're in on this team. You're in on that team. You're in on something else. You're in here but now you're moving to there.' It's one of those deals. That's why we try to use guys at different positions all through training camp, work them at different positions in practice. A lot of times on your punt team you have maybe one guy on the inside and he's the first guy in, so if you lose any of your interior people he'll be the first guy in and you bump somebody else over or he plays all the way across the board. And then you have your first gunner and then on the punt return maybe the same thing, one inside guy, one end, one vise guy, that type of deal. There are some moving parts there. It's definitely challenging."

KICKING-GAME SPECIALISTS

"It always comes down to the specialists. If your returners and your kickers and your snappers do a good job then you have a chance to be good. If they don't do a good job then it's hard for the other 10 guys to overcome that. It's hard to be a good punting team if you can't punt. It's hard to be a good return team if you can't return."

PUNTERS AS HOLDERS

The day when the backup quarterback was the holder on field goals and conversions largely has passed. For the Patriots and most other clubs, the punter now handles those duties. Ryan Allen and kicker Steve Gostkowski form a seamless combination, largely because they spend so much time together in special teams meetings and on the practice field.

"Most college teams have a pure snapper as well as a pure kicker and a pure punter. When you have that situation, if your punter can hold, then the amount of snaps and time that those guys get to practice together, work together, meet together, watch film together, watch slow-motion films, concentrate on the technique as opposed to the backup quarterback or somebody like that who has a lot of other responsibilities. If your holder can be your punter then the amount of practice time, consistency, preparation time that those guys have together just so outweighs what it would be with any other player.... If it's a position player like a defensive back and something happens to them, now who's your backup player because those guys are regular players? Not only do you have to replace them at their offensive or defensive position, you have to replace them in the kicking game so it cuts into your depth.

"Back when you had 36, 37 players, it was a whole different ballgame. Everybody doubled up in one way or another. I think that's the way it is on most teams. Most teams' punters are the holder and the snappers are the snappers and the kickers are the kickers. That's the way it was in college so we're recruiting players that are in that very specialized phase themselves."

RETURNING PUNTS VS. KICKOFFS

While the Patriots are reasonably productive in running back kickoffs and punts, they excel in bottling up opponents on returns. During the last couple of seasons their special teams have ranked among in the league's top four for fewest yards allowed.

"The big difference, of course, is on kickoff returns. You get a chance to build up your speed. You get a chance to handle the ball cleanly. There's nobody on top of you

Belichick fully focused, as always, during a 2007 training camp session. (photo by Barry Chin)

when you catch it, and you're able to run and set up your blocks and hit things full speed through that point, usually between the 20- and 30-yard line, the returner gets a chance to set those blocks up and hit them and try to get through there.

"The punting game is a lot more situational. On kickoffs the ball is always kicked from the same place. Rarely is there a difference. There are some but they're minimal, after a safety or that type of thing. But punting, the ball can be anywhere so the situation they're punting in can be quite diverse and sometimes complex.

Punters are very good at directional punting and kicking different types of punts—the end-over-end punts, spiral punts, spirals that don't turn over and so forth. So the ballhandling is a little more complex and you have to deal with players around you as you're catching the ball sooner or later.

"Sometimes a punter will outkick his coverage, but the majority of the time there's some decision-making involved. Whether to catch it and try to make the first coverage player or two miss to get the return started or fair catch it or to let it go and not catch the ball or to let it go over your head and let it go in the end zone for a touchback. So there's a lot of decision-making on just whether to catch the ball and whether to catch it and run with it or whether to catch it and fair catch it that are played different than the kickoffs. And then in addition to that, you deal with defenders and coverage players that are on you a lot quicker on punt returns, so sometimes you only have a yard or two or a couple yards to get into space, make a guy miss, break a tackle, whereas the kickoff is much more of a buildup play.

"Because they're so different a lot of times you don't have the same player doing both. Because they're so different I find the two plays fascinating and intriguing and a great part of the strategy of football…. That's why I take an opposing view to the people who want to eliminate kickoffs from the game. I think it's an exciting play. It's a unique play and one that is a big momentum play because of what happened the play before. The score or possibly the two times at the start of the half where it's a tone-setter or a pacesetter for that opening play. They're played different and, of course, the same thing in the blocking. You get a chance to set up a return whereas on the punting side of it you have an option of trying to pressure the punter and block it or return it, but you have to return it from the line of scrimmage.

"You can't drop off too far because of the possibilities of fakes, so you have to keep enough guys up at the line of scrimmage to ensure that the ball is punted. You have to ensure that you don't get onside-kicked to but that's much less frequent and the rules are in the kick returner team's favor on the onside kick. So it's a big gamble for the kicking team to do that as a surprise tactic. So the blocking patterns and techniques of blocking are quite different on the punt returns compared to what they are on kickoff returns."

RETURNING KICKOFFS

"A big part of it is certainly judging the ball. The flight of the ball, the timing of the return, the judgment coming out of the end zone. There are so many kicks in the NFL that are in the end zone—even the ones that are brought out a lot of times are multiple yards deep. So there's all those judgments. Then there's understanding how to set up the blocks on the blocking pattern of the return. It's not just running to daylight.

"Wherever [the returner] goes, everybody else goes to, so it's being able to set up the blocks for the front line so that they can keep leverage on the defenders and then he can cut off them. When you're blocking on a kick return, if you don't know where the runner is then that's really hard for you to put yourself in position between yourself and the defender to make the block if he runs different directions. But if he runs to a certain point, then you can position yourself so that you can get between your man and where he's going to end up.

The coach in purposeful stride during the 2013 camp. "We don't have forever." (photo by Jim Davis)

"Maybe that's where he's going and maybe that's where he starts but then the play and the design is to run somewhere else and you're able to position yourself between the man and where the runner is. So there's a discipline and a timing and a setting of those blocks up that's important for those guys to get. Whether they get that in college, I don't know. I just know that the fundamental of a good kickoff returner is to be able to handle the ball cleanly, have explosive speed and decision-making, set up the blocks, and then, when there's a seam, get through it."

RETURNING FROM THE END ZONE

"You're seeing guys come out from seven, eight, nine, nine-and-a-half yards deep now that you probably wouldn't have seen a while back.... When you tell a kicker to just bang away, sometimes those kicks that are coming down seven, eight yards deep in the end zone have a 3.8 [second] hang time, too. So it's not the same. There's a difference between two yards deep and four or five hang time and nine yards deep and 3.8 hang time. I'd rather be nine yards deep. There's a trade-off there and I think the returners are definitely aware of that. The guys that are going for distance, trying to touchback it, yeah, the balls are deeper, but many of them are with less hang time and sometimes significantly less hang time. That changes it, too. It's not all about how deep the ball is. There's certainly a hang time element involved as well."

SHORT KICKOFF RETURNER

"That's definitely a key role on the team. It's like the personal protector on the punt team. It's the last line of defense for the returner…. Sometimes he cleans up on blocks. Sometimes he's assigned to a specific guy, but usually he would have to weave his way through some traffic, like the wedge or another coverage player to get to his assignment. You don't want him blocking the first guy down because there would be too much penetration. Normally he's on more of a second-level player or he's looking to take some kind of leakage. If [it's] a right return maybe he takes the leakage from the left side so that nobody catches the returner from behind. But he has to make that decision of 'Is the guy close enough or can we bypass him and go to somebody else?'

"That all gets into the relationship between him and the returner and the track that the returner is on. Being able to know where he is, know who you have to block, who you don't have to block, and then making decisions in terms of getting to your man through traffic so that you can get to your assignment without screwing the returner up. I'd say there's definitely a lot to that position. It's a hard position to play. It's kind of a combination of being the fullback in the running game but you're dealing with a lot more space and lot more decision-making. Sometimes those guys are reading three, four, five different people on one play, depending on what happens."

KICKING AWAY FROM RECEIVERS

"The most important thing for us is our field position at the end of the play and how far out we can get the ball for our offense to take over. That's the goal, not who handles it or any of that. What's our starting field position? We just try to maximize whatever those opportunities are. Wherever the kick goes, that's something we can't control. Once it's kicked we can handle it properly, make the right adjustments, and have returns that are more favorable or advantageous for those types of kicks. You can't necessarily always count on that.

"It's like golf, it's situational. Sometimes you're trying to kick it to the left or kick it to the right. Hang time's more important than distance. The quickness of getting the punt off is more important than the distance on it and so forth and so on. There's a lot of situational punting that plays into the return game as well. If they situationally kick you, whether it be directionally or mortar kicks or squib kicks or overload the coverage with the kick and all those kinds of things, then those plays are a little different than other plays where they just kick it in a more conventional fashion…. So we always have to work on those and be ready for them. We know we're going to get them, potentially, from any team. Kicking's not just how far you can kick it and in the return game it's not just how far they kick it to you. There's a lot of other things that play into it."

PUNT RETURNERS

"A punt returner can't be watching the guys run down the field when he's catching the ball. But while the ball is in the air there's a short amount of time, a second or two, when he can start to get an idea of how the coverage is getting displaced, as opposed to a kickoff return where everybody is in their lane and starts down the field. On the punt team by the time the ball is snapped and the blocking occurs and guys get off the line it's not usually just the wave of guys.

"There is some kind of displacement in the coverage. You can get a feel for what kind of depth the gunners have. A good returner takes the ball off the punter's foot, sees it start to pick up the flight in the air, takes a look at how the coverage is starting to unfold and come down the field and get a sense of what the opportunities might be. Then, as the ball is coming in he has to get a feel for how close or how dangerous those guys are to hitting him when he catches the ball, whether to fair catch it and that type of thing.

"So, a lot of decision-making there in a pretty short amount of time. Some of that depends on what the return is and what we're trying to set up and what we're trying to do. There's definitely a lot of judgment and decision-making involved there, no question.... Sometimes it's better to make no decision than make the wrong one... sometimes you're better off just getting away from the ball rather than trying to catch it in traffic or catch it on the run or put yourself in a spot where you could lose the ball."

IDENTIFYING POTENTIAL PUNT RETURNERS

"Put them back there and watch them catch them. Eventually that's what it comes to. You put them back there, see how they handle the ball, coach them a little bit. The flight of the ball, teach them how to read the kick and so forth, how it's going to break and whether it's long, short, breaking left or right, whatever it happens to be. If they show promise then keep working with them.... It's like a lot of other skills. It can be developed, it can be improved. It doesn't mean it happens with everybody, but

Belichick at ease during Super Bowl week before the 2015 showdown with Seattle. (photo by Jim Davis)

it could if a player has good skills for it, if he has good judgment, can handle the ball. I mean, that's the biggest thing, is the ball handling.

"Kickoff returns, there's no one on you for the most part so you have plenty of time to catch the ball. You're not under pressure to make the decision as to whether to fair catch it or to catch it. You might make a decision if you want to bring it out of the end zone or not but that's different than actually handling the ball with guys around you and having to deal with them almost as soon as you touch the ball. Catching the ball and judging the ball, especially here—we're not playing in a dome—so every kick is a little bit different based on the wind and the way the ball comes off the punter's foot and so forth. That's a big skill for a punt returner, is just ball judgment and ball handling and decision-making. Whether to catch it, fair catch it, let it go, so forth. A lot more decision-making involved there so that really is experience. The ballhandling is not a natural thing because it can be improved, but to some degree it's a natural thing."

PUNTING VARIABLES

"Punting is a lot different than kicking off. There's not a lot of kickoff situations, usually. You're just trying to kick the ball high and deep, like standing out there on the driving range with your driver. But punting, it's a whole different ballgame. You know, where you're punting the ball 50 yards plus. Do they have eight guys up? Do they have six guys up? What's the rush look like? How does that affect the ball handling? How does that affect the return where you're trying to place the ball based on wind, based on possibly the defensive alignment? Are they one deep or two deep? Is there a key on where the return is going to go? Do you want to kick away from their returner? There's a lot of things that go into just punting the ball. Put the ball down on the 35-yard line for a punt and there's a lot of things that go into that play, more so than kicking off."

PUNT COVERAGE

"Every punt is different. There's a six-man box, there's a seven-man box, there's an eight-man box, there's an overloaded box. Who are the edge rushers? What's the field position? What's the down and distance? Who's the returner? The wind, the return tendencing… are they vising [double-teaming] the gunner? Are they vising both gunners? Do they have a key guy that sets the return that's the point-of-attack guy in the return game? Are we going to kick away from him or whatever the case may be? Who are their game-plan rushers? How do we handle guys coming off the gunners? The corner roles, the fake corner roles and all of that. The personal protector is a critical guy in all of that…. Everybody up front being on the same page, being able to pick up all of the different twists and having to involve a guy with his head between his legs as a blocker, especially when they put good rushers on that guy. That's usually where you get one of their best guys, so the challenge of snapping and blocking but also helping that guy with his block because he can't see. And if they twist when he's snapping the ball, which they do, then other people have to come in play there.

"So it's really a great team play. The gunners not only making tackles but downing balls and playing with proper leverage and getting the ball to the other coverage players so they can be effective.... It's a game within a game, it really is. It's a one-play situation, but if you punt seven or eight times in a game probably five of them are going to be unique. One or two might repeat. You might have a second plus-50 punt or a second backed-up punt with the same direction or the same wind or whatever it is. But there's a lot of variety in those plays and the later it goes in the game then the more it becomes a situational game. A lot of times the yards aren't that important. Whether it's 35 or 40—it's nice if it's 40 but that's not the most important thing. The most important thing is that it's not minus-20."

PERSONAL PROTECTOR

"He has several important jobs. The personal protector handles the communication on the punt team in terms of protection. If they bring eight players up to potentially rush the punt with the two other guys covering the gunners, you would have to block eight and you've got to get that right. You want to block that in the most advantageous way for your punt team, so making the calls as to how to handle the protection, who's going to take who, who's going to go where, and if that number diminishes, whether it goes from eight to seven to six.

Belichick exulting after the destruction of Denver in their 2011 divisional playoff game at Gilette. (photo by Jim Davis)

Or sometimes there's six guys in there, like five-and-one guy stacks.

"When you have more people than they do you can organize it so you can try to create a free guy. You have eight guys there. Which guy do you want to try to get free? So it's kind of a quarterback of the punt team… there is a lot of communication and decision-making in terms of protection and organizing the coverage from a blocking standpoint. He is the last line of defense, so that is another important decision. When to release into coverage, when to stay a little bit longer and protect the punter, when to leave his guy to get somebody else who may be more dangerous—that maybe a blocker had missed in front of him—and those kind of things."

BLOCKING FIELD GOALS

"Back in the '70s, you had the jumpers, you had the Matt Blairs and the guys like that that would have five, six, seven blocks a year. That was eliminated. The center is probably the weakest by far protector on any team's field goal unit but you're not allowed to hit him. You can't line up on him so that's another opportunity you don't have. You can't overload, so you can only put six guys to a side. You don't have that extra guy to create that extra gap, so you can't do that. You can't push anybody from behind.

"I'd say it's a lot harder because you have a lot less options. And on top of that, the kickers are better. The surfaces are much, much better. You don't have some of the bad fields where it was hard just to kick the ball, period. The baseball stadiums and the infield that got sodded and all that. You're not dealing with those kind of situations. Kicking off the dirt, you don't see that any more. The kickers have gotten better and the conditions have gotten much better and you're not allowed to do a lot of things that you would normally do to try to block a kick. So, yeah, it's gotten harder."

CHAPTER 9

Strategy

WHILE BILL BELICHICK JUSTIFIABLY IS RENOWNED AS A master strategist adept at turning a game's pivotal points in his team's favor, much of his acumen comes from his relentless focus on the present. "What's important to us is this game and our preparation for this game and our performance in this game," he said.

The Patriots prepare meticulously for each week's opponent, paying particular attention to individual matchups, to how rival players may be neutralized, and to positions where the rival lacks depth.

At the same time, following the club's Next Man Up approach, the coaching staff makes sure that every player is ready to step in whenever circumstances call. "Anyone could be out after one or two plays," observed Belichick. "You don't want to be drawing up stuff on the sideline."

While the game plan is tailored to what the staff expects is most likely to work, Belichick has conditioned his assistants and players to react to whatever is happening in the moment and to go off script as needed.

"When it comes down to situational football at the end of the game, that's where you need to make the plays you need to make to win," Belichick said. "We prepare for those plays, but which ones come up? It's only a handful of them and ultimately those are the ones you have to make."

LIVING IN THE PRESENT

"I don't believe—and our team doesn't believe—in living in the past. We can go back and look at a million things that have happened in every game. That's not really important to us. What's important to us is this game and our preparation for this game and our performance in this game. That's what we're all focused on and that's what we will be focused on. Next week it will be next week. There's certainly things that have happened in other games that we learn from. We learn from every game. We address things that we feel like need to be addressed, that we need to learn from and then we move on and attack the next situation."

BULLETIN-BOARD MOTIVATION

While Patriot players usually are aware of what's being said about them by upcoming opponents, Belichick discourages them from returning fire. "We don't engage," linebacker Marquis Flowers said before last year's AFC title game. When receiver Wes Welker made puckish references to stories about Jets coach Rex Ryan's reported foot fetish before a playoff game, Belichick benched him for the opening series. The players' generic response to rivals' gibes: "We'll see on Sunday."

"You can go in there and beat your helmet against your locker before you go out on the field... but as soon as the ball is snapped, you do your job better than they do theirs or vice versa. After a couple of plays, it might be after one play, it is really about execution. What team

Owner and coach savoring a successful season before the Super Bowl victory over the Seahawks. (photo by David Ryan)

can do what they have to do better than the other team? Not just individually one-on-one, but collectively as a group. You get into situational football, field position, clock management, changing personnel groups, substitutions, calls, and adjustments. That to me is what the game is about.

"You can go in there, take a sledgehammer, and break up the cinder blocks, but I don't think that helps you block them. I don't think that helps you tackle them. I don't think it helps you do what you need to do from a football standpoint. If you can't do that then I think the rest of it is minimal. I think in general what we all need to do is focus on what our jobs are and do that. There are a lot of potential distractions out there, stuff gets said and we all know what kind of stuff happens. Sometimes they can be distracting. I am not saying that we don't feel them or it isn't a burr in your saddle, but in the end you have to put all of that past you, whether you are on the giving or receiving side. I have seen it go on both ways. Go out and do your job. That is really what it comes down to."

ALL-AROUND BALANCE

"You always want to be balanced in your game. The most important thing is to make the plays you need to make to win. What plays are those going to be? I don't know. I'm not sure. But do you want to have good balance between your running game and passing game, production in your kicking game, production on defense, winning the turnover ratio, winning the field position battle, and all those things that lead up to it? Of course. You want to have the edge in all those categories. That just helps the whole flow of the game. Sometimes it works out that way, sometimes it doesn't. Sometimes you have an advantage in one area and the opponent has an advantage in another area.

"In the end it comes down to a few plays at the end of the game on anything—kicking a field goal, blocking a field goal, a pass, defense, whatever it is. When it comes down to situational football at the end of the game, that's where you need to make the plays you need to make to win. We prepare for those plays, but which ones come up? It's only a handful of them, and ultimately those are the ones you have to make."

SCORING POINTS ACROSS THE BOARD

"You don't go into a game thinking that, well, we're going to score a touchdown on a fumble return or we're going to score a touchdown on a kickoff return or something. You don't go into a game thinking that, because you're lucky if you get three or four of those through the entire course of the season. If you get one a month you're probably doing well…. You don't really count on a blocked kick for a touchdown. You're lucky if you get one of those a year. League-wide, when you look at all of the averages, that would put you very high up there if you had one of those.

"When you score like that, they're points that you really don't count on, so to get them is a bonus. It's a plus and obviously it's great to get them. It's great awareness by the team that executes it, whether it's the special teams or a defensive player or a turnover or whatever it is. They're good points to get. I don't think you can ever count on them: 'We're going to score on a punt return in a game.' How many of them are there? But when you get them it's tough and when you give them it's hard to overcome those. It's another possession that you have to have and that you have to get just to neutralize the points that you've given up when they didn't have the ball. You have to not only score once to neutralize that, but then you would have to score again just to have an advantage based on that miscellaneous return or miscellaneous score, whatever it is. An interception, fumble return, blocked kick, however it shows up."

BEING ON THE SAME PAGE

"Football is a team sport. You want everybody to be on the same page doing the right thing, whatever that is. We're a lot better off as a team if we're all wrong together than if half of us are right and half of us are wrong. We're better off all playing the same thing even if it's not what we should be in, than half in one thing and half in something else. That's what communication is, making sure that when the ball's snapped, when the play's run, whichever side of the ball we're on, that we're all consistent doing the same thing. Then at least you have a chance. Once you're in one of those half-and-half deals it's almost impossible to tie it together properly."

SITUATIONAL ROLES

"When I first came into the league you just didn't have as many personnel groups as you have now. A lot of times those 11 guys never left the field. Like the Hail Marys from Roger Staubach back in the '70s, it's just their regular offense, a guy running a go route. It wasn't all those guys together jumping it and tipping it and that type of thing. You rarely saw a tight end. You saw two receivers, you saw two backs, whatever. You had four backs—those four replaced those two, those two replaced the other two. If you had two tight ends then your tight end replaced the other tight end. There were no two–tight end sets.

"Even in goal-line, short-yardage on the 1-yard line, you still usually had two spread receivers. There was no third receiver. There were a few teams that played nickel defense like the Redskins when George Allen was there but it wasn't really nickel. It was just the defensive back came in for a linebacker. They played the exact same thing but it was just a DB instead of a linebacker having those coverage responsibilities. Maybe he was a little more athletic and had a little more coverage skill. If something happened to him they would put their linebacker back in and just run the same thing.

"It wasn't until the late '70s to early '80s when you had teams running two tight ends and one back and even starting to get into three receivers. I remember being with the Giants in '81 and we didn't even have a nickel defense. That was a big step. I can't remember what year it was, maybe it was '82 or '83, and we were like, 'Okay, we're going to put the nickel in this year.' It was like, 'Oh my God, this is going to be a big step, how are we going to do this?'

"Now there are more players but you have three receivers, you have two–tight end sets, you have your five, maybe six DBs, you've got your pass-rush guys. You've got your backup punter, you've got your 50-plus punter, you've got your short–field goal kicker, you've got your field goal snapper, you've got a punt snapper, you've got an onside kick guy, you've got four tight ends on this formation, you've got four, five wide receivers on this formation.

Belichick examining photo printouts during last year's preseason loss to the Jaguars. (photo by Barry Chin)

It's just more and more substitutional groups. If you have more and more players it gets further away from just the 11 guys that you had out there.

"You can take it all the way back to the '50s in college football, when you didn't have free substitution. Guys went both ways. You look at some of the old defenses there. Why were teams playing a 5–3 and a 6–2? Because it was the same guys who had to play offense. You had to take your offensive players and put them on defense. Or, more importantly, you had to take your defensive players and then fit them onto offense. If a lot of fullbacks looked like guards it's because they were linebackers on defense. The game, in terms of substitution and all that, has expanded tremendously."

EXPLOITING OPPONENTS' LACK OF DEPTH

"We definitely try and do that. We try to take an assessment of the team after you've had time to do it. Let's call it by the end of the first quarter, just to pick a time. How's it going? It looks like they're having trouble here or it looks like so-and-so isn't very effective. Or maybe a defensive player will come off and say 'So-and-so, I don't think he can run.' or 'I don't think he has the stopping quickness that he had the last time I played him.' They tell us that.

"A lot of times they see it before we do. Sometimes if we know about it, we try to have people on our staff that observe that and take an assessment of where they are to confirm it with the players. Maybe there's something you can do about it, maybe there isn't. Maybe it's just that individual matchup of how that person plays them that can be used to some advantage, as opposed to some big scheme thing like, 'Okay, this player's limited in something. What play do you want to run?' Maybe it's less of that and more of, 'Okay, we're competing against this player. This looks like a weakness today. Here's how individually we want to block him or defend him or whatever the case may be.'"

NEUTRALIZING OPPOSING PLAYERS

"The fundamentals of any matchup are, when you look at a player you see his strengths and you also see his weaknesses. You say, 'Okay, this is what he does well but this is what he doesn't do so well, and this is how we can attack that player or neutralize him.' Every player has things, especially in this league, that they do well and then they have things that they don't do so well. Or you can hopefully match up a player on them where you think that player can be competitive because of the way that they match up.

"That's what we try to focus on. If guys do something well, then how do we neutralize it? How do we stalemate that? And then how do we take advantage of something that maybe they don't do quite as well as other players we've played? Or maybe our skills are a little bit better than theirs in a certain area. We have more quickness, we have more size, we have more power. They don't block moving targets as well or they don't block stationary targets. Whatever it is, we try to work that angle. That's why each one of those individual matchups across the board is important, whether it be the receivers and defensive backs or the linebackers and the tight ends and the backs or the linemen. Those are all key matchups for us every week."

MATCHUPS

"The easiest thing in the world is for one player to match another. 'Okay, you go cover this guy.' All right, great. But what do the other 10 guys do? That's the problem. It's easy to match up one guy. That's simple. What do the other 10 guys do? What if he's here? What if he's there? What if he goes in motion? What if he's in the backfield? What if it's this personnel? What if it's that personnel in the game? Then how does all of the rest of it match up? That's where it gets tricky. You can be spending all day, literally, on that. Now if [the guy] is always in the same spot, then it's a lot easier in terms of scheme to match up and make your adjustments and so forth.

"Again, there are a lot of different ways to match up. You can match up and put your best guy on their best guy or you can match up and put your best guy on their second-best guy and put your second-best guy on their best guy and double him. If you're going to put your best guy on their best guy and double him anyway, then you lessen the matchups down the line. It's like setting a tennis ladder. If you put your bad guy at 1 and you win 2 through 7, great. If you put your best guy at 1 and he gets beat by their 1 and then your 2 versus their 2, that's what you're doing. You have a three-to-four-man ladder there with the receivers and your DBs, except we don't have to match them that way. You can match them however you want."

DEFERRING COIN TOSS

In 2008, the rule was changed to allow the coin-toss winner to defer the option to kick or receive to the second half. In all but two of the subsequent 50 games, the Patriots chose to defer. They opted otherwise in the 2017 regular season finale against the Jets and the divisional playoff with the Titans, electing to receive. In the Super Bowl, they deferred, and the Eagles received and drove down for a field goal.

"There is something to be said for setting the tone offensively and going out there, first drive and all that.

If you have received the opening kickoff, now you start the second half and say, "Okay, they are going to take the ball.' Then you really have a decision to make relative to the wind, if that is a factor. Do you have it in the third quarter when you are kicking off, or do you want it in the fourth quarter when the passing and kicking game might be a little more important? I think it is the reverse of that when you defer. You have the opportunity for two possessions, one at the end of the half and one at the start of the third quarter, so there is a chance for that back-to-back possession and then you don't always have that third-quarter decision.

"If you defer, then you take the ball and take the wind at the start of the game, then the second half it puts the

The coach preparing assiduously for the 2011 season—in April. (photo by Stan Grossfeld)

ball in their court as far as that wind decision goes, which is always a tough one. Whatever you decide to do on that you are always giving some consideration to the other side. 'Do I want it in the third or do I want it in the fourth?' It certainly has made it more of a decision than it was in the past. Unless you were playing in a hurricane you just automatically take the ball. Now there are some things to consider and I do think there is a certain comfort level with just taking the ball."

SCRIPTING OPENING PLAYS

"The thing that you have to take into consideration is the situations. Do you want to call the same play on first-and-15 that you want to call on second-and-1? Do you want to call the same play on third-and-6 that you want to call on second-and-4? If you follow the script then, 'Okay, here's the fourth play.' But would you really want to call that play in that situation or would you rather call your second-and-short play in second-and-short and your third-and-long play in third-and-long? It's a couple of different philosophies on that. There's merit to both of them.

"I've done it both ways. At times we've said, 'Okay, this is what we want to do sequentially.' Other times we've said, 'The first time it's second-and-long, this is what we're going to call. The first time it's second-and-short this is what we're going to call.' It's not the same play. I think there is a place for both. It's really a philosophy of either how you want to start the game or how you want to start a particular game with your sequence of call. That's usually an end-of-the-week decision—Thursday, Friday, Saturday. You've practiced everything. Here's how it looks. Here's what our comfort level is of calling the plays with our players and our team and then you make the decision of, 'Okay, this is what it's going to be.' Last year [2009] against Baltimore we started off the game and recovered a fumble and we got the ball at the 15-yard line. So what play do you want to call there? The first play of your script or your 15-yard play or your first play after a turnover? You've got to decide how you want to handle those situations because it isn't always that clean when it comes up."

GAME PLANNING AND INJURIES

"Whatever your game plan is you've got to be able to run with whoever you have in the game. Anyone could be out after one or two plays. You don't want to be drawing up stuff on the sideline. So whatever you're going to run, you have to have somebody to back up everybody to run it. You've got to have a backup right tackle, a backup right guard, a backup tight end, a backup running back, a backup receiver. Somebody takes reps at those positions during the course of the week. Now if you lose two guys at the same position, I don't care what position it's at, you're probably talking about some adjustments. You lose two centers, you lose two corners, you lose two linebackers, you lose two of anything then I would say 90 percent of the time that would be a pretty good scramble. To lose one guy to any position, you've got to be prepared for that. That's football."

FOCUS WHILE CHALLENGING PLAYS

The rules allow teams to make two challenges per game on calls that they believe are questionable. Coaches, who toss a red flag onto the field as a signal, are required to issue their challenge before the next play. "Incontrovertible visual evidence" is required to reverse a call. If a challenge fails, the team is charged with a timeout.

"I don't think you can wait to challenge the play. If you're calling the play, you have to call the play. You can't wait and [think], 'Is there going to be a replay? What's going to [happen?]' You can't operate like that…. The person up in the press box that relays that information says, 'Okay, the ball is spotted. It's inside the one or it's on the one-and-a-half or wherever the ball is. Or it's first-and-goal if we've gotten a first down or it's third-and-one if we haven't gotten a first down, whatever it is.' Then you have to make your call.

"You can't wait. Now while all that's going on we would have somebody else who would be seeing if there is a replay and then they would tell me or I would say, 'Okay, Josh [McDaniel], we're going to challenge the play.' That type of thing. We're a little bit independent on that. As the play caller you have to see the situation, see what the down-and-distance is or what the field position is. Is it inside the 20? Is it inside the 10? Because maybe you have a breaking point on your calls there, possibly. Then you want to know what their personnel is. So if you're changing personnel you want to know what's in the game. Is nickel in or did they stay regular? Or did they come in with dime or whatever it is?

"As soon as you get that information, then you make your call. You can't have five people talking at once. You get the information from the press box as quickly as we can see it. The ball is on the two, it's second down, here comes nickel. Then, all right, you make your call. Or sometimes they hold their subs until you make your subs. Here comes goal-line, whatever it is. As soon as you make your call you say, 'Okay, give me whatever it is—give me three receivers. Three receivers start on there and then as the call is being made the person in the press box says, 'Here comes nickel.

Or here comes dime. Or they're staying regular.'Then he'll finish making his call because that might affect what he's calling. It might not, but it might. Meanwhile, the whole replay thing is separate from that."

KEEPING OPPONENTS GUESSING

"When somebody does that [an unusual formation] to you, you've got two reactions to it. One is, if it was successful, 'Until we stop it they might do it again,' or 'They did that this time, they'll probably do something else the next time.' And you could be right or wrong. So that's part of the challenge of game planning. It's no different with anything else, either. It's not just a player in a different position. It could be a formation or a play. So you run a play that works or a formation that you can see gives them trouble with an adjustment and then you're at the next game and what do you do?

"Do you go back and do the same thing and say, 'Well, they couldn't handle it, let's do it again?' Or do you say, 'Well, they're going to be working on that. Let's go to something else.' And sometimes you can out-dumb yourself by going to something that hasn't worked and giving up on something that has. And sometimes you can out-dumb yourself by doing the same thing every time, knowing they're spending the whole week on it and not moving on to something else…. Every team does things differently from another team. We do things differently than Buffalo did them. New Orleans does things differently than Miami did them.

"Everybody is different and you've got different players, so the game-planning decision ultimately comes down to how much do you want to do what you do and how much of what somebody else does can you apply? Or, how much of what somebody else does do you want to try to shift and do what they do? And then, what kind of problems does that bring for you? Yeah, you can do what somebody else did, but if they were very familiar with it and they knew how to adjust it and they know how to handle different problems that come up within it better than you do, then it's a good idea but you can't go out there and execute it, which in the end is really what it comes back to: What can you execute? We can draw up anything we want on the board: 'You guys go here, you guys go there.' But then when the play starts, can you actually get done what you need to get done?

"That's where it comes down to execution. In the end that's more important than the Xs and Os. You can put the Xs and Os wherever you want them but if you can't do it, then what good is it? So you've got to be able to execute where you put them and depending what your system is and where you place them and what changes you make, sometimes you can, sometimes you can't. But you've got to decide how much you want to commit to that. If you want to change from what you do to what somebody else did in another game, you've got to decide how big of a change that is and then how well you can actually do it."

DIRECTIONAL KICKING

"Directional kicking is like anything else. It's a strategy. There are some advantages to it and there are some drawbacks to it. One of the advantages is you can shrink the field and put the ball in a certain location and that can be good. The drawbacks to it are [that] it creates a lot of

Belichick does have more than one expression. But this banner, visible behind the End Zone Militia's celebratory musket fire at Gillette Stadium, displays his default version. (photo by Barry Chin)

field somewhere else so if they bring it all the way across the field you are defending a lot more space. So if you kick it long enough or low enough or they can hold you up long enough to get back there sometimes you don't solve a problem, sometimes you create one.

"It is hard to tell your coverage players to all go to one spot because you can't always get the ball kicked to where you want it. It is hard enough to kick the ball high, long and straight. Now you are talking about hitting the corner of the green, carry the bunker and all of that. Well, if the ball is not over there and you send everyone over there and the ball ends up down the middle or, God forbid, out of bounds on a kickoff…. It is hard to place the ball perfectly right where you want it in the punting game and even on kickoffs. You can sometimes favor a side, but it is not 100 percent that the ball is going to be over there.

"How much do you commit your coverage when you kick it that way? And then if it is not kicked that way you are outnumbered or you are outflanked. Any time you try to directionally kick—let's say to the short side of the field—sooner or later those teams are going to try to test you out and come back to the big side, the long field, and if the ball is not all the way over there and you happened to have that on, you could really be giving up a big one. There are some good things to it. It has a place both on kickoffs and punts but it has some downsides, too. You have to either do it very well or pick your spots. Sometimes when we play here or in Buffalo, because of the wind, whether you want to directional kick or not, you are directionally kicking. You don't have any control over it. It is just too much. That changes the game a little bit there and it probably shortens the field, too, because the ball just doesn't travel as far."

IDENTIFYING YOUR OWN TELLS

"One of the best places to start is with your teammates. So we work against each other each day and what a good teammate will do, a defensive player will tell an offensive player, 'Hey, I can tell when you're pulling. I can see your depth.' An offensive player would tell a defensive player, 'I can tell when you're blitzing,' or 'We see a man-coverage stance or a zone-coverage stance. In zone, your feet are here. When you're in man, it's a little bit different.' A lot of it starts on the practice field.... If one of our players can pick it up, you've got to assume that one of their players watching film can pick it up, if it's a stance or a mannerism or whatever it is.

"I know that the quarterbacks do that with the secondary and the defensive coaches will do that with the offensive coaches, especially in training camp, but sometimes even in the scout team stuff. We talk about what the quarterback saw. How did he know this was going to happen? Or somebody tipped it off. Or, how did the defense know that this was going to happen? Well, because they're not threatened by something else. We haven't run this kind of complementary play to it and that's why it's being overplayed by a guy in practice. So we definitely try to watch ourselves, but I think on the practice field or on practice film there's a good give-and-take there between the staff and the players to try to help each other."

Belichick consults with offensive coordinator Josh McDaniels during the 2017 training camp. (photo by Jonathan Wiggs)

PLAYING AGGRESSIVELY
WITHIN THE FRAMEWORK

"You want to be aggressive. You want to be able to take advantage of those opportunities that you can get a little jump on the play without giving them up, without exposing yourself, without putting yourself in a vulnerable position either as a team or as an individual player. We do the same thing; that's what coaches do. You try to make calls that give you an opportunity to be aggressive and take advantage of something without having too much exposure. Just in case they don't do that, then what's the downside? What's going to happen if they do something else? Are you going to get strip-sacked? Are you going to get hit for a 10-yard loss? How aggressive do you want to be? How much do you want to try to push the envelope on that?

"It's a coaching-scheme thing. It's also individual player decision-making on each play. It's complicated. It gets into matchups. If a guy is covering one guy you play it one way. You're covering somebody else, you might play it a little bit differently. You're blocking one guy, you're thinking a little bit more of this. You're blocking another guy, you might not think quite as much of that. That changes within the game, where people move and so forth. Part of being a football player is making those kinds of decisions. That's what instinctive, good players do. They make the right one."

PREPARING FOR UNPREDICTABLE PLAYS

"If you have a team that has a history or some type of trend of doing a certain thing then you hit it that week for sure because it's on your checklist. But procedurally there are a thousand plays that can happen at the end of the game. We can't practice every one of those plays every week. Same thing in the kicking game. There are a hundred situations that if the play comes up once a season it would be a lot. But they come up so you hit those on an infrequent basis but try to make sure that you cover them so if it does come up you know how to handle it."

NO-HUDDLE ADJUSTMENTS

"Sometimes after you've been through a no-huddle situation or even a two-minute drive, the players and the coaches, we're standing on the sideline and have had eight or nine plays and, in all honesty, some of them are running together. Whereas at the normal pace, most of the time if you say, 'Hey, what happened on that play?' the player will say, 'Well, here's what happened,' and they know the play and they know the situation you're talking about and all of that. In a no-huddle they're saying, 'On that play, what happened? Did that? Did he? Did he pass protect or did he fake and then check out?' 'What play are you talking about now?' They just run eight or nine plays together. So defensively and offensively it does put a little bit more stress on your sideline. Just the pace of the game.

"It's third down and your punt return team has got to be ready, your field goal block team has got to be ready, depending on where it is. Then all of a sudden you're back out there playing on a first-down call. So it can happen pretty quickly. It just means that everybody's got to be alert and they're a lot more used to it than we are because they've been doing it on a weekly basis."

BALL SECURITY

Leaving a ball on the ground is a certain way for a Patriot back or receiver to find himself back on the bench. In three of the last four seasons, the club has ranked second in least fumbles made and consistently recovers more than it loses.

"In the end it's the players' ability to secure the ball and their dedication to protecting it. There's some turnovers that when you watch the play you say, 'Well, there wasn't much we could do to prevent that.' There are other ones that you could do more to prevent and so you just hope that every player will do everything he can when he has the ball to secure it and take care of it. There's going to be some plays where a defender comes in and has a perfect hit with his helmet right on the ball, and there's enough pressure on the ball that will jar it loose from just about anybody. And then there's other plays where there's almost no pressure on the ball and it comes out. The same thing with interceptions. Sometimes the defenders make great plays and you look at it and say, 'Boy, that was a tremendous play!' And then there's other times you look at it and say, 'Boy, that could have been prevented with a better route, a better throw, better protection, whatever happened on that play.' You try to avoid the ones that are just careless."

TWO-MINUTE OFFENSE

Under Belichick, the Patriots have been masterful at scoring in the final two minutes of the first half. Last season they managed it 14 times, including in both AFC playoff games, and also did it six times in the second half, including game-winning scores against the Texans and Steelers. The Eagles turned the tables on them in the Super Bowl, though, tallying scores late in each half.

"The two-minute at the end of the half is a lot different than the two-minute at the end of the game. They're two completely different situations. I know everybody talks about them like they're the same but to me they're not anything the same. You don't have to score at the end of the half. If you have to score at the end of the game to win the game then that's a totally different situation. If you have to score, to get in position to kick a field goal or score a touchdown to win or tie the game, then that's a totally different situation than at the half, when if you don't score at the end of the half you haven't lost the game.

"Do you want to score? Sure. You want to score every time you have the ball. That's why you put the offense out there. If you don't want to score you just send the punt team out there. We're always trying to score but it's different at the end of the half. You try to take what you can get and not put yourself at more risk than you have to. At the end of the game you have to do whatever you have to do to move the ball and get it in position to win the game. So you have to take chances.

"You have to do things you may not want to do in order to have an opportunity to make plays you need to make. That's dictated by the situation. Field position is part of it but so is everything else—time, timeouts, how you match up in that situation. I think it's all part of it. There are a lot of factors in that, in what you call and what happens in the sequence of plays that you call. Each one is different. Obviously there are some common threads but I think each situation each week is different based on the matchups and based on whatever the specific situation is—time, timeouts, field position, playing conditions, et cetera."

HAIL MARY PASSES

"I think it's not an overly strategic play. You want to get the ball in the end zone and get people around it, however you orchestrate that. I mean, you don't want to throw it short and you don't want to throw it out…. Trying to get the ball to somebody that has a chance to go up and fight for it and then having other people there to rebound the ball if it comes up. Defensively, it's sort of the reverse of that. You've got to have somebody go up and you don't want to get out-jumped for the ball. Then you never really get a shot at it. But at the same time you want to be able to box out and keep the other players who don't go up and jump for it from coming down with the rebound."

CHAPTER 10

Art & Science

BILL BELICHICK BEGAN COACHING IN AN ERA OF blackboards, erasers, and 60-millimeter film. The modern day of digital technology and iPads baffles him. "If the TV's busted some people can walk in there and fix it. I look at it, all I see is wires," he said. "TV, VCR, Sirius radio, whatever it is. It all looks the same to me."

But since the Patriots players are comfortable with 21st century methods of learning, Belichick and his assistants have changed how they impart information. "We've converted as a coaching staff and as an organization to what's better for the students," he said, "than what's better for the teachers."

But while Belichick acknowledges the value of high-tech modes of instruction, he stresses that the fundamental things still apply. "In the end," he said, "you have to go out there and play football."

OLD-SCHOOL TECHNOLOGY

"You think about people like Paul Brown and Vince Lombardi and Sid Gillman and every picture I think of them as next to a projector with the film running. I still have a lot of films in my personal possession. I have nothing to watch them on. There's been obviously a huge change. Film technology and the whole teaching and being able to do cut-ups, and I do something and I can share it with somebody else. If somebody else does the work they can share it with me. The communication and the flow of information is incredible, nothing that I would have ever envisioned in 1975 when I was working with the Colts."

HOLE-PUNCH TECHNOLOGY

"I'm totally overwhelmed by [modern technology]. Without somebody holding my hand and helping me through it there's no way I could get a fraction of what I get. When we were with the Colts, I wrote every play on a card. I drew the card, I drew the play, and then every category that the play fit into I checked off alongside the outside edge of the card. If it was first-and-10, plus-territory, gain of over four yards, screen pass, halfback was the receiver, the defense ran a blitz—whatever categories

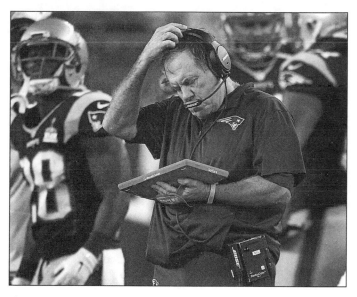

The 60-millimeter man puzzling over modern technology. "I look at it, all I see is wires." (photo by Jim Davis)

it fell into, then I would check those off. I would take the hole punchers, so there were like 200 holes around the edge of the card, and I would punch out the holes that I had checked off. Then you have a whole stack of cards here, slide the ice pick back in there, and all the screens fall out, or whatever you're looking at.

"So, okay, 15 screens and you look at them. How many were strong? How many were weak? How many to the halfback? How many were play-action? How many were on third down? How many were on second down? Figure that out and stack them back in there again. I would do like 200 of those—screens and third down and red area and goal line and short yardage and what they ran against blitzes and what they ran from slot and what they ran from motion and all that. That's about as archaic as you can get, the ice-pick method. But it worked."

TECHNOLOGY EVOLUTION

"One of the biggest things I've learned through my coaching career is the evolution of learning and the evolution of technology and the tools that I came into the game with in 1975. I mean, our team wouldn't even recognize what those things are—a projector and 60-millimeter film and chalk and erasers. We don't even have that stuff any more. We progressively go on to different types of technology. I'd say the thing I've learned is that other people don't learn the way I learned. I'm not comfortable with some of that technology, but they are and they can learn better with the newer technology than I can because I'm not used to it. But it's their method of learning. They've been using it all their lives.

"So we've converted as a coaching staff and as an organization to what's better for the students than what's better for the teachers. As teachers we've had to adjust, we've had to learn, which has been good for us, too—me in particular. A lot of our coaches, I think they're a lot

better at this than I am, that's for sure. We've had to adjust
to new methods of technology, teaching, apps, and differ
ent things that we're not familiar with that our players are
that will help them. The tablets and those kind of things
are certainly convenient. Guys can be getting treatment in
the training room and they can be watching their tablet.
It's a lot easier than when I came into the league when
you had to take a projector and a roll of film home and
watch it. Now everybody has it, they have the access to
it. Or before when we had to take our film and put it on
VHS—not that any of our players would know what a
VHS is. Then they would pop it into their TV and watch
it. Of course, you couldn't rewind it. That's what we had
to work with.

"So we progressively worked through those stages.
Now we're into another stage. It's been very educational
for me. I've leaned on a lot of our IT people, like [IT
specialist] Dan Famosi has done a tremendous job in
coordinating all of this. But also our coaches who have
used it with other teams or other organizations they've
been in or it's been brought to their attention that this is
how another team is doing it. Then one of our coaches or
scouts or whoever it is will go and find out how somebody
else is doing it and see how we can apply it to us. But Dan
has been the guy for us that's just taken all that stuff to
the level that we're at. Just daily handling all the moron

coaches like me that can't turn it on or can't get from one view to another, to our players and just the compatibility and accessibility of all the information."

SEEING THINGS

"If the TV's busted some people can walk in there and fix it. I look at it, all I see is wires. TV, VCR, Sirius radio, whatever it is. It all looks the same to me. It's just a bunch of wires and if it doesn't work, if I hit the button and it doesn't turn on, that's it. There're other people that come in there and boom, boom, boom, everything works. The computer works, the TV works, the VHS works, everything, perfect. Some people have a capacity to see things. Some people have trouble with math, some people have trouble with the English language. I have trouble with both of them. There're all different strengths and weaknesses. You coach players, some guys see things, they see everything. Some guys, they see nothing."

THE FUNDAMENTALS

"I'm sure we have enough technological equipment in here to put the whole team on the moon. In the end it comes down to blocking and tackling and running and throwing and catching and kicking and solid fundamentals and all that. You could put the iPad on the super-duper wizard computer and whatever you want. You could throw all that crap on there and I'm sure you could get some statistical analysis that would provide 28 theses for MIT. In the end you have to go out there and play football. I wouldn't lose too much sight of that. Same thing in baseball. [Former manager] Tony La Russa and I, we've talked about that a lot, too. You have to throw the ball, you have to hit it, you have to catch it, you have to field it, you have to run the bases. You could go out there and talk about some guy's batting average when the count is 2-1 at night. I mean, sooner or later you have to go out there and play."

Belichick as he appears in your living room. (photo by Yoon Byun)

MORE STUFF

"The more stuff there is, the more stuff there is that can go wrong. But when it works, it's great. Great line from Curley in the Stooges. He gets in the car and says, 'Hey, what's wrong with this car? I don't know, it seems fine. The clock is working.'"

CHALLENGING PLAYS

"The easiest challenge is when you look at the play on the screen and it's obvious to you that the play was called incorrectly. That's no problem. The harder one is when you see the play with your own eyes and you say, 'I don't think that's the way it should have been called,' but can you find another picture of it that confirms what you actually saw? That's the question. And then there are the plays that maybe you think you have a 25 percent chance of being right on. 'Maybe we could get this. I doubt it.' But it's such a big play in the game and you maybe don't need your timeouts. It's the end of the first half or something and your timeouts aren't critical at that point, then maybe you take that lesser percentage chance and say, 'Okay, we didn't see the play, we didn't get a real good look at it but we think it's close. Let's take a shot at it.' Was his arm going forward? Was the ball out? Was it a fumble? Was it an incomplete pass? That kind of thing. It doesn't get replayed up there but it's a big play in the game, then maybe you just take a shot at it and say, 'I hope it comes out in our favor.'"

TRICK PLAYS

"One of the worst ones that I ever ran was in '79 against the Rams when I was the special teams coach on the Giants. We went out to play L.A. in the Coliseum and we didn't have a real good team. It was Phil Simms' rookie year and Dave Jennings was one of our best players, All-Pro punter. I mean, he was great and he could throw. He was a very athletic guy, so we had several fake punts that we hit. And unfortunately we were punting a lot, so that gave us more opportunities than we needed. Brian Kelley was a fullback, so we snapped the ball to Kelley and he ran a sweep. Once he was about to get tackled he stopped, turned, and lateraled it back to Jennings on the other side of the field.

"The play didn't work very well. It wasn't very well executed and when Jennings caught the ball he thought he had a chance to get the first down but he really didn't. But he thought he did, so he ran for the sticks there on the sideline and then about three guys hit him about four yards short of the first down, knocked him out of bounds. I mean, he got knocked over by the cheerleaders. His helmet was on sideways, he's looking out through the ear hole. The ball is out there on the track somewhere and [head coach] Ray Perkins looks over at me with that look of 'What are we doing? This is our best player.' He [Jennings] looked like he got run over by two Mack trucks. So we go all the way over to the other side of the field and get him off the track and put him back together again. He got killed. And then Ray said—which I would have done the same thing but I wouldn't have done it as nicely as he did—'Look, we're not running any more fakes like that again. Just forget that.' He didn't put it quite that way, but you get the idea."

CHAPTER 11

Hoodie on Holidays

HALLOWEEN

BILL BELICHICK: "Got your Halloween costume ready?"

FRIDAY WARRIORS: "Any plans for a costume?"

BB: "Yeah. I'll be a ghost. Got your candy ready? What are we giving out this year?"

FW: "Pez."

BB: "Pez? With the dispenser? Good."

FW: "Do you have a favorite type of candy?"

BB: "Yeah, all of them. Remember when you were a kid and you went back to the house that had good candy twice? And then they threw you out, like, 'Hey, you've been here. Get out of here.' Or you hope that everybody didn't show up at your house and there was some left over. Those were the days."

Belichick and longtime girlfriend Linda Holliday enjoying a Celtics game in 2009. (photo by Barry Chin)

FW: "What was your best Halloween costume?"

BB: "I kind of lucked into it. It was John Kennedy. It was easy. You dress up and you put on the mask. But it was during the Cuban missile crisis, as it turned out. I think I won the prize there. Everybody was really impressed that the president was able to break away from the Cuban missile crisis to attend a Halloween party—a school Halloween party…. What could be a better holiday than costumes and candy? How can you go wrong? Whoever came up with that—that was brilliant."

FW: "What's your favorite Halloween candy?"

BB: "Whatever is in the bag. I like them all, whatever you drop in there."

FW: "No costume?"

BB: "No, no."

FW: "No pirate?"

BB: "This is it. I'm in it."

CHRISTMAS

BILL BELICHICK: "How are we doing here? Christmas shopping done? Started? Yeah, I'm with you. We're on the same schedule…. Did you get your Christmas shopping done? I just finished up mine this morning. You've still got some time."

FRIDAY WARRIORS: "What did you get me?"

BB: "It's in the mail."

BILL BELICHICK: "Good morning. How are we looking today? Got everything that you asked Santa for?"

FRIDAY WARRIORS: "How about you?"

BB: "Yeah, no complaints, no complaints."

CHAPTER 12

Bill in Brief

AS VOLUBLE AS BILL BELICHICK CAN BE DURING HIS Friday press conferences, he can revert to his laconic "We're on to Cincinnati" mode, particularly when the topic is his Hall of Fame quarterback. And while all questions produce answers, some can be one sentence long.

Q: "I know what the answer to this question is, but I have to ask it."

A: "So why are we going to ask it, then?"

Q: "Do you expect Tom Brady to play this weekend?"

A: "We'll list Tom on the injury report like we always do, like everybody else. Is that the answer you were hoping for?"

Q: "Not hoping for, but expecting."

A: "Okay, good. I don't want to disappoint you."

Q: "What are your thoughts on Tom Brady rejoining the team?"

A: "He never left."

Q: "Do you anticipate Tom Brady will practice today?"

A: "We'll list his status at the end of practice."

Q: "What was he able to do yesterday?

A: "Play quarterback. The usual thing."

Q: "Did he practice?"

A: "He did just the way we listed him. That's what we do after every practice."

Belichick pointing westward before the divisional playoff at San Diego on January 14, 2007. (photo by Jim Davis)

Q: "He wasn't injured during the week, though? Because he was listed as non-injury on Wednesday."

A: "I think we covered that. I think we've already talked about that."

Q: "It was a planned day off? It wasn't that he was hurt during practice, right?"

A: "I think we've covered that."

Q: "Will he be able to play in the game?"

A: "It's all been covered."

Q: "Now that Brady is dealing with this injury do you have any regrets about trading Jimmy Garoppolo?"

A: "We're getting ready for Jacksonville."

Q: "Does it look like Brady's playing status might be a game-time decision?"

A: "Today's Friday."

Q: "Why do you prefer the running back-by-committee approach?"

A: "I prefer scoring and winning. That's my preference."

Q: "Have you ever thought about how much more entertaining it would be for us if you had a style more like Rex Ryan's?"

A: "You're not the first guy to mention that."

Q: "Do you run out of the room when they're on TV talking about how great you are?"

A: "I don't see a lot of that."

Q: "Will you request anything from Giants Stadium when it is torn down?"

A: "No, I don't think so. They will still be digging through looking for Jimmy Hoffa's body."

Q: "You mentioned a clean slate. Can you give your rationale for the redecorating and taking all the pictures down?"

A: "The walls needed painting."

Q: "Daylight savings a few weeks ago. Did you get your clock all figured out?"

A: "Yeah, still working on that, yeah."

Q: "For those of us who weren't there last night, can you update us on why Vince Wilfork didn't play?"

A: "We just didn't put him in. That's why."

Q: "Because?"

A: "Because there were other players who played."

Q: "How has Jonathan Fanene done?"

A: "He's been here one day."

Q: "We're just trying to follow up and be thorough."

A: "That's one thing about you guys. You can be thorough, especially on certain subjects, absolutely. I'm not being critical. I'm just stating the facts."

Q: "How much did you play yourself and what were your limitations?"

A: "Pretty much everything. Size, speed, athletic ability."

The coach in silhouette before the Super Bowl date with the Falcons. (photo by Jim Davis)

Q: "Did you happen to notice the 'Cheaters Look Up' banner yesterday and what was your reaction to it?"

A: "I don't know what you're talking about."

Q: "Have you heard about that plane?"

A: "What plane?"